Risk Quantification and Allocation Methods for Practitioners

ATLANTIS STUDIES IN COMPUTATIONAL FINANCE AND FINANCIAL ENGINEERING

Series Editor: Prof. Argimiro Arratia

ISSN: 2352-3115

This book series aims at expanding our knowledge of statistical methods, mathematical tools, engineering methodologies and algorithms applied to finance. It covers topics such as time series analysis, models of financial assets and forecasting, algorithmic trading, high-frequency trading, portfolio optimization, risk management, machine learning and data analysis in financial applications.

We welcome books that balance theory and practice of financial engineering and computational finance, combining formalism with hands-on programming exercises.

Books in "Atlantis Studies in Computational Finance and Financial Engineering" will all be published in English and all book proposals submitted to this series are being reviewed by key experts before publication. We offer the reader a rigorous view of the state of the art and new perspectives in computational finance and financial engineering.

Risk Quantification and Allocation Methods for Practitioners

Jaume Belles-Sampera, Montserrat Guillen,
and Miguel Santolino

Atlantis Press / Amsterdam University Press

Cover design: Coördesign, Leiden
Lay-out: Djilali Boudiaf
Printed and bound by CPI Group (UK) Ltd, Croydon, CR0 4YY

Amsterdam University Press English-language titles are distributed in the US and Canada by the University of Chicago Press.

ISBN	97 94 6298 405 9
e-ISBN	978 90 4853 458 6
DOI	10.5117/9789462984059
NUR	916

Preface

This book aims to provide a broad introduction to quantification issues of risk management. The main function of the book is to present concepts and techniques in the assessment of risk and the forms that the aggregate risk may be distributed between business units. The book is the result of our research projects and professional collaborations with the financial and insurance sectors over last years. The textbook is intended to give a set of technical tools to assist industry practitioners to take decisions in their professional environments. We assume that the reader is familiar with financial and actuarial mathematics and statistics at graduate level.

This book is structured in two parts to facilitate reading: (I) Risk assessment, and (II) Capital allocation problems. Part (I) is dedicated to investigate risk measures and the implicit risk attitude in the choice of a particular risk measure, from a quantitative point of view. Part (II) is devoted to provide an overview on capital allocation problems and to highlight quantitative methods and techniques to deal with these problems. Illustrative examples of quantitative analysis are developed in the programming language R. Examples are devised to reflect some real problems that practitioners must frequently face in the financial or the insurance sectors. A collection of complementary material to the book is available in http://www.ub.edu/rfa/R/

Part (I) covers from Chapters 1 to 5. With respect to risk measures, it seemed adequate to deepen in the advantages and pitfalls of most commonly used risk measures in the actuarial and financial sectors, because the discussion could result attractive both to practitioners and supervisor authorities. This perspective allows to list some of the additional proposals that can be found in the academic literature and, even, to devise a family of alternatives called GlueVaR. Chapters in this part are structured as follows:

Chapter 1 - Preliminary concepts on quantitative risk measurement

This chapter contains some preliminary comments, notations and definitions related to quantitative risk assessment to keep the book as self-contained as possible.

Chapter 2 - Data on losses for risk evaluation

A descriptive statistical analysis of the dataset used to illustrate risk measurement and allocation in each chapter of the book is here presented.

Chapter 3 - A family of distortion risk measures

A new family of risk measures, called GlueVaR, is defined within the class of distortion risk measures. The relationship between GlueVaR, Value-at-Risk (VaR) and Tail Value-at-Risk (TVaR) is explained. The property of subadditivity is investigated for GlueVaR risk measures, and the concavity in an interval of their associated distortion functions is analyzed.

Chapter 4 - GlueVaR and other new risk measures

This chapter is devoted to the estimation of GlueVaR risk values. Analytical closed-form expressions of GlueVaR risk measures are shown for the most frequently used distribution functions in financial and insurance applications, as well as Cornish-Fisher approximations for general skewed distribution functions. In addition, relationships between GlueVaR, Tail Distortion risk measures and RVaR risk measures are shown to close this chapter.

Chapter 5 - Risk measure choice

Understanding the risk attitude that is implicit in a risk assessment is crucial for decision makers. This chapter is intended to characterize the underlying risk attitude involved in the choice of a risk measure, when it belongs to the family of distortion risk measures. The concepts *aggregate risk attitude* and *local risk attitude* are defined and, once in hand, used to discuss the rationale behind choosing one risk measure or another among a set of different available GlueVaR risk measures in a particular example.

Part (II) covers from Chapters 6 to 8. Capital allocation problems fall on the disaggregation side of risk management. These problems are associated to a wide variety of periodical management tasks inside the entities. In an insurance firm, for instance, risk capital allocation by business lines is a fundamental element for decision making from a risk management point of view. A sound implementation of capital allocation techniques may help insurance companies to improve their underwriting risk and to adjust the pricing of their policies, so to increase the value of the firm. Chapters in this part are structured as follows:

Chapter 6 - An overview on capital allocation problems

There is a strong relationship between risk measures and capital allocation problems. Briefly speaking, most solutions to a capital allocation problem are determined by selecting one allocation criterion and choosing a particular risk measure. This chapter is intended to detect additional key elements involved in a solution to a capital allocation problem, in order to obtain a detailed initial picture on risk capital allocation proposals that can be found in the academic literature.

Personal notations and points of view are stated here and used from this point forward. Additionally, some particular solutions of interest are commented, trying to highlight both advantages and drawbacks of each one of them.

Chapter 7 - Capital allocation based on GlueVaR

This chapter is devoted to show how GlueVaR risk measures can be used to solve problems of proportional capital allocation through an example. Two proportional capital allocation principles based on GlueVaR risk measures are defined and an example is presented, in which allocation solutions with particular GlueVaR risk measures are discussed and compared with the solutions obtained when using the rest of alternatives.

Chapter 8 - Capital allocation principles as compositional data

In the last chapter, some connections between capital allocation problems and aggregation functions are emphasized. The approach is based on functions and operations defined in the standard simplex which, to the best of our knowledge, remained an unexplored approach.

Acknowledgements

The origins of the present book go back five years ago, when J. Belles-Sampera began doctoral studies supervised by M. Guillen and M. Santolino at the Faculty of Economics and Business of the University of Barcelona (UB). We are grateful to the colleagues of the UB Riskcenter research group for their fruitful discussions that undoubtedly improved the manuscript. We also thank the members of the jury Jan Dhaene, José María Sarabia and Andreas Tsanakas, for their comments and suggestions.

We thank the team at Atlantis Press for their assistance in the publication process, particularly to Keith Jones, Debora Woinke and Zeger Karssen. We are grateful to Argimiro Arratia, series editor of Atlantis Studies in Computational Finance and Financial Engineering, for his valuable comments on preliminary drafts of this book. We acknowledge AGAUR SGR2014-001016 and the financial support of the Spanish Ministry for grants ECO2013-48326-C2-1-P, ECO2015-66314-R and ECO2016-76302-C2-2-P. Montserrat Guillen also acknowledges ICREA Academia.

Contents

List of Figures

List of Tables

PART I

RISK ASSESSMENT

1 Preliminary concepts on quantitative risk measurement

This chapter is structured in two parts. The first one is intended to compile a set of theoretical definitions that we consider useful and relevant for quantitative risk managers. These definitions are related to the quantitative risk assessment framework of unidimensional risk factors, so other key issues like multivariate dependence are not covered herein. In our opinion, the concepts addressed in this chapter are the building blocks of unidimensional risk measurement which need to be helpful to practitioners. A careful first reading of this part is not necessary if one is already familiar with the fundamental ideas, because our aim is to leave it as a reference point to which to go back whenever needed. The second part serves to introduce ideas to bear in mind when moving from theory to practice. As before, this selection is subjective and it relies on our judgment, and the reader could consider the subjects in this selection too specific or too obvious. This is also the reason why we close the chapter with some brief remarks, in which we provide additional topics to be aware of and selected references in the literature to become an expert on risk quantification.

1.1 Risk measurement - Theory

1.1.1 First definitions

Definition 1.1 (Probability space). A probability space is defined by three elements $(\Omega, \mathscr{A}, P)$. The sample space Ω is a set of all possible events of a random experiment, $\mathscr{A}$ is a family of the set of all subsets of Ω (denoted as $\mathscr{A} \in \wp(\Omega)$) with a σ-algebra structure, and the probability P is a mapping from $\mathscr{A}$ to $[0, 1]$ such that $P(\Omega) = 1$, $P(\varnothing) = 0$ and P satisfies the σ-additivity property.

Some remarks regarding the previous definition. $\mathscr{A}$ has a σ-algebra struc-
ture if $\Omega \in \mathscr{A}$, if $A \in \mathscr{A}$ implies that $\Omega \smallsetminus A = A^c \in \mathscr{A}$ and if $\bigcup_{n \geqslant 1} A_n \in \mathscr{A}$ for
any numerable set $\{A_n\}_{n \geqslant 1}$. Additionally, the σ-additivity property afore-
mentioned states that if $\{A_n\}_{n \geqslant 1}$ is a succession of pairwise disjoint sets belonging to $\mathscr{A}$ then

$$P\left(\bigcup_{n=1}^{+\infty} A_n\right) = \sum_{n=1}^{+\infty} P(A_n).$$

A probability space is finite, i.e. $\Omega = \{\omega_1, \omega_2, \ldots, \omega_n\}$, if the sample space
is finite. Then $\wp(\Omega)$ is the σ-algebra, which is denoted as 2^{Ω}. In the rest
of this book, N instead of Ω and m instead of ω are used when referring
to finite probability spaces. Hence, the notation is $(N, 2^N, P)$, where $N = \{m_1, m_2, \ldots, m_n\}$.

Definition 1.2 (Random variable). Let $(\Omega, \mathscr{A}, P)$ be a probability space. A
random variable X is a mapping from Ω to $\mathbb{R}$ such that $X^{-1}((-\infty, x]) := \{\omega \in \Omega : X(\omega) \leqslant x\} \in \mathscr{A}, \forall x \in \mathbb{R}$.

A random variable X is discrete if $X(\Omega)$ is a finite set or a numerable set
without cumulative points.

Definition 1.3 (Distribution function of a random variable). Let X be a random variable. The distribution function of X, denoted by F_X, is defined by
$F_X(x) := P\left(X^{-1}((-\infty, x])\right)$. The notation $P(X \leqslant x) = P\left(X^{-1}((-\infty, x])\right)$
is commonly used, so expression $F_X(x) = P(X \leqslant x)$ is habitual. The distri-
bution function of a random variable is also known as the cumulative distribution function (cdf) of that random variable.

The distribution function F_X is non-decreasing, right-continuous and satisfies that $\lim_{x \to -\infty} F_X(x) = 0$ and $\lim_{x \to +\infty} F_X(x) = 1$.

Definition 1.4 (Survival function of a random variable). Let X be a random variable. The survival function of X, denoted by S_X, is defined by
$S_X(x) := P\left(X^{-1}((x, +\infty))\right)$. The following notation is commonly used, $P(X > x) = P\left(X^{-1}((x, +\infty))\right)$, so expression $S_X(x) = P(X > x)$ is habitual. So,
the survival function S_X can be expressed as $S_X(x) = 1 - F_X(x)$, for all $x \in \mathbb{R}$.

The survival function S_X is non-increasing, left-continuous and satisfies that
$\lim_{x \to -\infty} S_X(x) = 1$ and $\lim_{x \to +\infty} S_X(x) = 0$. Note that the domain of the distribution function and the survival function is $\mathbb{R}$ even if X is a discrete ran-
dom variable. In other words, F_X and S_X are defined for $X(\Omega) = \{x_1, x_2, \ldots, x_n, \ldots\}$ but also for any $x \in \mathbb{R}$.

Definition 1.5 (Density function). A function f defined from $\mathbb{R}$ to $\mathbb{R}$ is a *density function* if $f \geqslant 0$, if it is Riemann integrable in $\mathbb{R}$ and if the following equality holds:

$$\int_{-\infty}^{+\infty} f(t)dt = 1.$$

A random variable X is absolutely continuous with density f_X if its distribution function F_X can be written as $F_X(x) = \int_{-\infty}^{x} f_X(t)dt$ for all $x \in \mathbb{R}$. Let us remark that, in such a case, the derivative function of F_X is f_X, so $dF_X(x) = f_X(x)$.

If X is a discrete random variable such that $X(\Omega) = \{x_1, x_2, \ldots, x_n, \ldots\}$ then for if $x \in \{x_1, x_2, \ldots, x_n, \ldots\}$, the density function may be defined by $f_X(x) = P(X = x_i)$ and $f_X(x) = 0$ if $x \notin \{x_1, x_2, \ldots, x_n, \ldots\}$.

Apart from discrete and absolutely continuous random variables there are random variables that are not discrete neither absolutely continuous but belong to a more general class. These random variables are such that their distribution function satisfies that

$$F_X(x) = (1-p) \cdot F_X^c(x) + p \cdot F_X^d(x) \tag{1.1}$$

for a certain $p \in (0,1)$, and where F_X^c is a distribution function linked to an absolutely continuous random variable and F_X^d is a distribution function associated to a discrete random variable X^d with $X^d(\Omega) = \{x_1, x_2, \ldots, x_n, \ldots\}$.

Definition 1.6 (Mathematical expectation). Three different cases are considered in this definition.

Discrete case

Let X be a discrete random variable with $X(\Omega) = \{x_1, x_2, \ldots, x_n, \ldots\}$. X has finite expectation if $\sum_{i=1}^{+\infty} |x_i| \cdot P(X = x_i) < +\infty$. If this condition is satisfied then the mathematical expectation of X is $\mathbb{E}(X) \in \mathbb{R}$, where $\mathbb{E}(X)$ is defined by

$$\mathbb{E}(X) = \sum_{i=1}^{+\infty} x_i \cdot P(X = x_i) = \sum_{i=1}^{+\infty} x_i \cdot f_X(x_i).$$

Absolutely continuous case

Let X be an absolutely continuous random variable with density function f_X. X has finite expectation if $\int_{-\infty}^{+\infty} |x| \cdot f_X(x)dx < +\infty$. If this condition is

Table 1.1   Examples of random variables

Type of r.v.	Name of r.v.	Distribution function
Discrete	Binomial, $X \sim B(m, q)$	$F_X(x) = \sum_{k \leq x} \binom{m}{k} \cdot q^k \cdot (1-q)^{m-k}$
Absolutely continuous	Normal, $X \sim N(\mu, \sigma^2)$	$F_X(x) = \int_{-\infty}^{x} \frac{1}{\sigma\sqrt{2\pi}} \cdot \exp\left\{ -\frac{1}{2\sigma^2} \cdot (t-\mu)^2 \right\} dt$
Mixed	Mixed exponential	$F_X(x) = \begin{cases} 0 & \text{if } x < 0 \\[2mm] 1 - (1-p) \cdot \exp\{-\lambda \cdot x\} & \text{if } x \geq 0 \end{cases}$ The probability of $\{X = 0\}$ is equal to $p \in (0, 1)$, the probability of $\{X < 0\}$ is zero and strictly positive values have assigned a probability of and exponential r.v. of parameter $\lambda > 0$, additionally multiplied by $1 - p$.

satisfied then the mathematical expectation of X is $\mathbb{E}(X) \in \mathbb{R}$, where $\mathbb{E}(X)$ is defined by

$$\mathbb{E}(X) = \int_{-\infty}^{+\infty} |x| \cdot f_X(x) dx < +\infty.$$

General case

Let X be a random variable with distribution function of the form (1.1), and such that

$$\begin{cases} p \cdot F_X^d(x) = \sum_{x_i \leq x} \left(F_X(x_i) - \lim_{t \to x_i, \, t < x_i} F_X(t) \right) = \sum_{x_i \leq x} P(X = x_i), \\[3mm] (1-p) \cdot F_X^c(x) = F_X(x) - p \cdot F_X^d(x) = \int_{-\infty}^{x} f_X^c(t) dt, \end{cases}$$

where $\{x_1, x_2, \ldots, x_n, \ldots\}$ is the set of discontinuity points of F_X. In this case, if the random variables linked to F_X^d and F_X^c respectively have finite expec-

Figure 1.1 Graphs of distribution and survival functions of random variables from Table 1.1, with parameters $m = 100$, $q = 5\%$, $\mu = 0$, $\sigma = 1$, $p = 70\%$ and $\lambda = 0.02$.

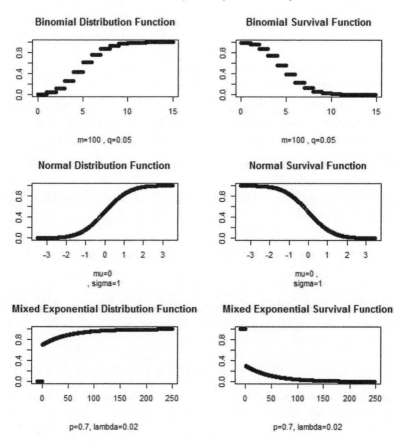

tation then

$$\mathbb{E}(X) = \sum_{i=1}^{+\infty} x_i \cdot P(X = x_i) + \int_{-\infty}^{+\infty} x \cdot f_X^c(x)dx.$$

Note that the differential function of a distribution function F_X, which will be denoted dF_X and is usually known as probability density function (pdf), may be defined by

$$dF_x(x) = \begin{cases} P(X = x_i) & \text{if } x \in \{x_1, x_2, \ldots, x_n, \ldots\}, \\ f_X^c(x) & \text{if } x \notin \{x_1, x_2, \ldots, x_n, \ldots\}, \end{cases} \quad (1.2)$$

Taking advantage of this notation, if the random variables involved have finite expectation then the mathematical expectation in the discrete, the absolutely continuous or the general cases can always be written as

$$\mathbb{E}(X) = \int_{-\infty}^{+\infty} x \cdot dF_X(x).$$

This expression unifies the ones used in Definition 1.6 and makes further reading easier than more complicated notation.

The following result will be really helpful in several parts of this book, although comments on its usefulness cannot be provided at this stage. The result shows how to interpret the mathematical expectation of a random variable in terms of its survival function.

Proposition 1.1. *Let X be a random variable with finite expectation. The following equality holds:*

$$\mathbb{E}(X) = \int_{-\infty}^{0} (S_X(t) - 1)dt + \int_{0}^{+\infty} S_X(t)dt. \qquad (1.3)$$

Proof. Each summand in (1.3) is treated separately, despite the idea behind the proof is basically the same. First of all, consider

$$a = \int_{-\infty}^{0} (S_X(t) - 1)dt \text{ and } b = \int_{0}^{+\infty} S_X(t)dt.$$

With this notation, $\mathbb{E}(X) = a + b$ has to be proved. In order to prove that, let us recall that $\mathbb{E}(X) = \int_{-\infty}^{+\infty} x \cdot dF_X(x)$ and rewrite this last expression as

$$\mathbb{E}(X) = \int_{-\infty}^{0} x \cdot dF_X(x) + \int_{0}^{+\infty} x \cdot dF_X(x) = a' + b'.$$

Using Fubini's theorem in $(*)$:

$$b' = \int_{0}^{+\infty} x \cdot dF_X(x) = \int_{0}^{+\infty} \left(\int_{t=0}^{x} dt \right) dF_X(x)$$
$$\overset{(*)}{=} \int_{t=0}^{+\infty} \left(\int_{x=t}^{+\infty} dF_X(x) \right) dt = \int_{t=0}^{+\infty} (F_X(+\infty) - F_X(t))dt$$
$$= \int_{t=0}^{+\infty} (1 - F_X(t))dt = \int_{0}^{+\infty} S_X(t)dt$$
$$= b.$$

$$a' = \int_{-\infty}^{0} x \cdot dF_X(x) = \int_{x=-\infty}^{0} \left(\int_{t=0}^{x} dt \right) dF_X(x)$$

$$\overset{(*)}{=} \int_{t=-\infty}^{0} \left(\int_{x=-\infty}^{t} (-dF_X(x)) \right) dt = \int_{t=-\infty}^{0} \left(\int_{x=-\infty}^{t} (dS_X(x)) \right) dt$$

$$= \int_{t=-\infty}^{0} (S_X(t) - S_X(-\infty)) dt$$

$$= \int_{t=-\infty}^{0} (S_X(t) - 1) dt$$

$$= a. \qquad \square$$

The proposition has been proved, using that $F_X(+\infty) = \lim_{x \to +\infty} F_X(x) = 1$, $S_X(-\infty) = \lim_{x \to -\infty} S_X(x) = \lim_{x \to -\infty} (1 - F_X(x)) = 1 - \lim_{x \to -\infty} F_X(x) = 1$ and $dS_X(x) = d[1 - F_X(x)] = -dF_X(x)$.

Definition 1.7 (Risk measure). Let Γ be the set of all random variables defined for a given probability space $(\Omega, \mathscr{A}, P)$. A risk measure is a mapping ρ from Γ to $\mathbb{R}$, so $\rho(X)$ is a real value for each $X \in \Gamma$.

Frequently, the set Γ is considered to be the set of p-measurable functions defined on the probability space, $p \geqslant 0$. In other words, frequently $\Gamma = \mathscr{L}^p\{(\Omega, \mathscr{A}, P)\}$. For more details see, for instance, Rüschendorf [2013] and the references therein.

The most frequently used, or well known, risk measures in the insurance and financial industry are listed in next paragraph. It has to be noted that insurance and financial perspectives may differ in some aspects. Detailed comments on these differences are provided in Section 1.2. Our perspective is the actuarial one and, hence, the following definitions are aligned with this point of view. In fact, these definitions are basically taken from Denuit *et al.* [2005]. The reason of including these definitions is to avoid possible misunderstandings due to differences in names given to certain risk measures.

Definition 1.8 (Value at Risk). Let us consider $\alpha \in (0, 1)$. The function

$$\text{VaR}_\alpha : \Gamma \longrightarrow \mathbb{R}$$
$$X \longmapsto \text{VaR}_\alpha(X) = \inf\{x \mid F_X(x) \geqslant \alpha\}$$

is a risk measure called *Value at Risk at confidence level* α. If F_X is continuous and strictly increasing then $\text{VaR}_\alpha(X) = F_X^{-1}(X)$, where F_X^{-1} is the inverse of the distribution function of random variable X.

Definition 1.9 (Tail Value at Risk). Let us consider $\alpha \in (0,1)$. The function

$$\text{TVaR}_\alpha : \Gamma \longrightarrow \mathbb{R}$$
$$X \longmapsto \text{TVaR}_\alpha(X) = \frac{1}{1-\alpha} \int_\alpha^1 \text{VaR}_\lambda(X) d\lambda$$

is a risk measure called *Tail Value at Risk at confidence level* α.

Definition 1.10 (Conditional Tail Expectation). Let us consider $\alpha \in (0,1)$. The function

$$\text{CTE}_\alpha : \Gamma \longrightarrow \mathbb{R}$$
$$X \longmapsto \text{CTE}_\alpha(X) = \mathbb{E}[X \mid X > \text{VaR}_\alpha(X)]$$

is a risk measure called *Conditional Tail Expectation at confidence level* α.

Definition 1.11 (Conditional Value at Risk). Let us consider $\alpha \in (0,1)$. The function

$$\text{CVaR}_\alpha : \Gamma \longrightarrow \mathbb{R}$$
$$X \longmapsto \text{CVaR}_\alpha(X) = \mathbb{E}[X - \text{VaR}_\alpha(X) \mid X > \text{VaR}_\alpha(X)]$$
$$= \text{CTE}_\alpha(X) - \text{VaR}_\alpha(X)$$

is a risk measure called *Conditional Value at Risk* at confidence level α.

Definition 1.12 (Expected Shortfall). Let be $\alpha \in (0,1)$. The function

$$\text{ES}_\alpha : \Gamma \longrightarrow \mathbb{R}$$
$$X \longmapsto \text{ES}_\alpha(X) = \mathbb{E}\left[(X - \text{VaR}_\alpha(X))_+\right]$$

is a risk measure called *Expected Shortfall at confidence level* α. Notation $(t)_+$ is used to refer to the function that returns 0 if $t \leq 0$ and t otherwise.

The following relationships between previous risk measures hold, as stated in Section 2.4 of Denuit *et al.* [2005]:

$$\text{TVaR}_\alpha(X) = \text{VaR}_\alpha(X) + \frac{1}{1-\alpha} \cdot \text{ES}_\alpha(X), \tag{1.4}$$

$$\text{CTE}_\alpha(X) = \text{VaR}_\alpha(X) + \frac{1}{S_X(\text{VaR}_\alpha(X))} \cdot \text{ES}_\alpha(X), \tag{1.5}$$

$$\text{CVaR}_\alpha(X) = \frac{\text{ES}_\alpha(X)}{S_X(\text{VaR}_\alpha(X))}. \tag{1.6}$$

Note that relationships (1.4) and (1.5) imply that, if the distribution function of random variable X is continuous and strictly increasing then TVaR_α $(X) = \text{CTE}_\alpha(X)$ because

$$S_X(\text{VaR}_\alpha(X)) = 1 - F_X(\text{VaR}_\alpha(X)) = 1 - F_X\left(F_X^{-1}(\alpha)\right) = 1 - \alpha.$$

This is the reason of finding expressions like: 'roughly speaking, the TVaR is understood as the mathematical expectation beyond VaR' in this book.

Example 1.1 (Illustrative exercise). Let us consider the following random variable X, that measures a loss, i.e. an economic value that can be lost with a certain probability,

x_i	-100	0	50	200	500
$p_i = P(X = x_i)$	0.2	0.5	0.25	0.04	0.01

a) Calculate $\text{VaR}_\alpha(X)$, $\text{TVaR}_\alpha(X)$ and $\text{CTE}_\alpha(X)$ for $\alpha = 90\%$ and for $\alpha = 99\%$.

b) Explain if a loss X which is distributed like in the table presented here can produce a TVaR at the 90% level that is equal to 180.

c) Find the value that must substitute 200 so that the results exactly correspond to $\text{ES}_{90\%}(X) = 13$, for a confidence level equal to 90%. Verify also that if we replace value 200 by 250 and value 500 by 550, then we obtain again the same results for a confidence level equal to 90%.

d) Based on the ideas in step c), explain why the value of the risk measures do not determine in a unique way the distribution of a random loss.

Solution **a)** In order to make calculations easier, we complete the initial table with two additional rows. One corresponds to the distribution function (cdf) of random variable X and the other is the corresponding survival function.

x_i	-100	0	50	200	500
$p_i = P(X = x_i)$	0.2	0.5	0.25	0.04	0.01
$F_X(x_i)$	0.2	0.7	0.95	0.99	1
$S_X(x_i)$	0.8	0.3	0.05	0.01	0

We calculate the values of $\text{VaR}_{90\%}(X)$ and $\text{VaR}_{99\%}(X)$ using Definition 1.8 $\text{VaR}_\alpha(X)$ and the information displayed on the table. So,

$$\text{VaR}_{90\%}(X) = \inf\{x \mid F_X(x) \geqslant 90\%\} = 50,$$
$$\text{VaR}_{99\%}(X) = \inf\{x \mid F_X(x) \geqslant 99\%\} = 200.$$

Both for the calculation of TVaR and CTE, we need to obtain the value of ES beforehand. Let us remind the definition of the latter for a loss random variable X and a confidence level $\alpha \in (0,1)$:

$$\text{ES}_\alpha(X) = \mathbb{E}\left[(X - \text{VaR}_\alpha(X))_+\right].$$

Note that we need to consider $Z_{X,\alpha} = (X - \text{VaR}_\alpha(X))_+$, which is equal to zero when $x_i - \text{VaR}_\alpha(X) \leqslant 0$ and which is equal to $x_i - \text{VaR}_\alpha(X)$ when the difference is positive. Let us add two more lines to the table that has been used in this exercise, corresponding to values $Z_{X,90\%}$ and $Z_{X,99\%}$:

x_i	-100	0	50	200	500
$p_i = P(X = x_i)$	0.2	0.5	0.25	0.04	0.01
$F_X(x_i)$	0.2	0.7	0.95	0.99	1
$S_X(x_i)$	0.8	0.3	0.05	0.01	0
$(x_i - 50)_+$	0	0	0	150	450
$(x_i - 200)_+$	0	0	0	0	300

Therefore,

$$\text{ES}_{90\%}(X) = \sum_{i=1}^{5}(x_i - 50)_+ \cdot p_i = 150 \cdot 0.04 + 450 \cdot 0.01 = 6 + 4.5 = 10.5,$$

$$\text{ES}_{99\%}(X) = \sum_{i=1}^{5}(x_i - 200)_+ \cdot p_i = 300 \cdot 0.01 = 3.$$

Once the values for ES are obtained, then we can calculate TVaR and CTE using the following expressions:

$$\text{TVaR}_\alpha(X) = \text{VaR}_\alpha(X) + \frac{1}{1-\alpha} \cdot \text{ES}_\alpha(X)$$

and

$$\text{CTE}_\alpha(X) = \text{VaR}_\alpha(X) + \frac{1}{S_X(\text{VaR}_\alpha(X))} \cdot \text{ES}_\alpha(X).$$

$$\text{TVaR}_{90\%}(X) = 50 + (1/0.1)10.5 = 155,$$

$$\text{TVaR}_{99\%}(X) = 200 + (1/0.01)3 = 500; \text{ and}$$

$$\text{CTE}_{90\%}(X) = 50 + (1/0.05)10.5 = 260,$$

$$\text{CTE}_{99\%}(X) = 200 + (1/0.01)3 = 500.$$

b) The random loss X that is considered in this exercise cannot correspond to another loss if some values of the risk measures at the confidence level of 90% are different to the risk measures obtained for the loss. For example, if the TVaR at the 90% level is 180 while we just saw that TVaR at the confidence level of 90% is 155 for the loss in this exercise, then the two random variables differ in their distribution.

c) Let us fix the level of confidence to 90%. Let us note in that case that the source of the difference between the risk measures TVaR and CTE in two cases is in the value of $\text{ES}_{90\%}(X)$. For instance if the value is 13, while it is 10.5 in section a) of the current exercise. Then, when looking at the calculation of $\text{ES}_{90\%}(X)$, what needs to be done is to look at the following equation:

$$(x_4 - 50) \cdot 0.04 + 450 \cdot 0.01 = 13, \text{ with } x_4 \geqslant 50.$$

Then, solving the previous equation, we obtain

$$x_4 = 25 \cdot [13 - 4.5 + 2] = 25 \cdot [10.5] = 262.5.$$

Furthermore, if we change $x_4 = 200$ by $x_4 = 262.5$ we obtain the results that we were aiming at, namely,

$$\text{VaR}_{90\%}(X) = 50, \quad \text{ES}_{90\%}(X) = 13, \quad \text{CVaR}_{90\%}(X) = 260,$$
$$\text{TVaR}_{90\%}(X) = 180, \quad \text{and} \quad \text{CTE}_{90\%}(X) = 310.$$

The variant proposed here is to consider now that x_4 equals 250 and x_5 equals 550, and leaving all other x_i as they were initially set. So, the value of $\text{ES}_{90\%}(X)$ is calculated as

$$(250 - 50)_+ \cdot 0.04 + (550 - 50)_+ \cdot 0.01 = 200 \cdot 0.04 + 500 \cdot 0.01$$
$$= 8 + 5 = 13.$$

Therefore, with this change, we obtain

$$\text{VaR}_{90\%}(X) = 50, \quad \text{ES}_{90\%}(X) = 13, \quad \text{CVaR}_{90\%}(X) = 260,$$
$$\text{TVaR}_{90\%}(X) = 180 \quad \text{and} \quad \text{CTE}_{90\%}(X) = 310.$$

d) In the previous paragraph, we deduce that at least, there are two random losses that have the same values for

$$\text{VaR}_{90\%}(X), \quad \text{ES}_{90\%}(X), \quad \text{CVaR}_{90\%}(X),$$
$$\text{TVaR}_{90\%}(X) \quad \text{and} \quad \text{CTE}_{90\%}(X).$$

As a consequence, we have just seen that the values of the risk measures do not determine in a unique fashion the cumulative probability function for a random variable.

1.1.2 Properties for risk measures

A list of properties that a risk measure may or may not satisfy is presented herein. Most of these properties have an economic interpretation or, at least, a relationship with some features that practitioners (the ones who want to quantify risk) demand to the risk measure (the instrument to quantify risk). In order to summarize the properties and their interpretation, Table 1.2 is provided.

Table 1.2   Properties for risk measures

Property	Idea behind the property
Translation invariance $\rho(X + c) = \rho(X) + c,$ $\forall c \in \mathbb{R}$	If a positive non random quantity c is added to random loss X then it is required to the risk measure that the risk value of the new loss should be increased by the same quantity. Otherwise, if the quantity c is negative (so a protection buffer has been added to the original random loss X) then the risk measure should reflect this buffer as a net effect on the original risk value.
Subadditivity $\rho(X_1 + X_2) \leqslant \rho(X_1) + \rho(X_2)$	If a risk measure satisfies this property then it is able to quantitatively reflect the idea that diversification is a strategy that does not increase risk.

Continued on next page

Table 1.2: continued from previous page

Property	Idea behind the property
Monotonicity $P(X_1 \leqslant X_2) = 1 \Rightarrow$ $\rho(X_1) \leqslant \rho(X_2)$	If losses of a position are almost surely worse than losses of another position, then the risk value of the former should be greater than the risk value of the latter.
Positive homogeneity $\rho(c \cdot X) = c \cdot \rho(X),$ $\forall\, c > 0$	If losses to which the risk manager is exposed are multiples of a particular loss, then it is required that the risk measure of the overall risk should be the same multiple of the risk value of that particular loss.
Comonotonic additivity X_1 and X_2 comonotonic $\Rightarrow$ $\rho(X_1 + X_2) =$ $\rho(X_1) + \rho(X_2)$	Informally, two random variables are comonotonic if they are linked to another random variable that drives their behavior. This property is intended to identify those risk measures that take into account this underlying relationship between comonotonic random variables and, as a consequence, they do not assign quantitative diversification benefits when considering the sum of those random variables.
Convexity $\rho(\lambda \cdot X_1 + (1-\lambda) \cdot X_2)$ $\leqslant \lambda \cdot \rho(X_1) +$ $(1-\lambda) \cdot \rho(X_2),$ $\forall\, \lambda \in (0,1)$	This is a sort of generalization of the subadditivity property. If the risk figure of any linear combination of two random variables is smaller than the associated linear combination of risk figures, then the risk measure captures diversification benefits in a continuous way. Note that if the risk measure is convex and positively homogeneous and considering $X_i' = 2 \cdot X_i$ and $\lambda = 1/2$, then the subadditivity property for X_i', $i = 1, 2$ is obtained.

Continued on next page

Table 1.2: continued from previous page

Property	Idea behind the property
Law invariance (objectivity) If $P(X_1 \leqslant x) = P(X_2 \leqslant x), \forall x \in \mathbb{R}$ then $\rho(X_1) = \rho(X_2)$	If two random variables have identical distribution functions then it is required to the risk measure that their risk values should be identical too.
Relevance If $X \geqslant 0$ and $X \neq 0$ then $\rho(X) > 0$	If a random loss is not zero then its risk value should be strictly positive.
Strictness $\rho(X) \geqslant \mathbb{E}(X)$	This property is intended to detect those risk measures that are conservative enough to be used as a management tool, in other words, risk values based in risk measures that satisfy this property are always greater that the expected loss.

For any random variables $X_1, X_2, X \in \Gamma$.

Financial and actuarial literature are plenty of interesting proposals of risk measures. Details on some of these proposals are provided in Chapters 3 and 4 and, in addition, several other references are pointed out therein.

1.2   Risk measurement - Practice

Let us start this section with Table 1.3, in which closed-form expressions are provided for VaR and TVaR where random variable X is distributed as a Normal ($\mathcal{N}$), a Lognormal ($\mathcal{LN}$) and a Generalized Pareto ($\mathcal{GP}$) distribution. Notation conventions are used. Namely, ϕ and Φ stand for the standard Normal pdf and cdf, respectively. The standard Normal distribution α-quantile is denoted as $q_\alpha = \Phi^{-1}(\alpha)$. For the $\mathcal{GP}$ distribution, the definition provided in Hosking and Wallis [1987] is considered, where the scale parameter is denoted by σ and k is the shape parameter. The $\mathcal{GP}$ distribution contains the Uniform ($k = 1$), the Exponential ($k = 0$), the Pareto ($k < 0$) and the type II Pareto ($k > 0$) distributions as special cases. Table 1.3 is basically taken from Sandström [2011].

Table 1.3   Analytical closed-form expressions of VaR and TVaR for selected random variables

Random variable	Risk measure	Expression
Normal distribution $\mathcal{N}(\mu,\sigma^2)$	VaR_α	$\mu + \sigma \cdot q_\alpha$
	TVaR_α	$\mu + \sigma \cdot \dfrac{\phi(q_\alpha)}{1-\alpha}$
Lognormal distribution $\mathcal{LN}(\mu,\sigma^2)$	VaR_α	$\exp(\mu + \sigma \cdot q_\alpha)$
	TVaR_α	$\exp\left(\mu + \dfrac{\sigma^2}{2}\right) \cdot \dfrac{\Phi(\sigma - q_\alpha)}{1-\alpha}$
Generalized Pareto distribution $\mathcal{GPD}(0,\sigma)$ (Exponential distribution)	VaR_α	$-\sigma \cdot \ln(1-\alpha)$
	TVaR_α	$\sigma \cdot [1 - \ln(1-\alpha)]$
Generalized Pareto distribution $\mathcal{GPD}(k,\sigma)$ with $k < 0$	VaR_α	$\dfrac{\sigma}{k}\left[1 - (1-\alpha)^k\right]$
	TVaR_α	$\begin{cases} +\infty & \text{if } k \leqslant -1 \\ \dfrac{\sigma}{k}\left[1 - (1-\alpha)^k\right] + \dfrac{\sigma}{k}\left[\dfrac{k \cdot (1-\alpha)^k}{k+1}\right] \\ \qquad\qquad\qquad\quad \text{if } k \in (-1,0) \end{cases}$

1.2.1   'Liability side' versus 'asset side' perspectives

No matter if you come from the insurance or from the financial industry: in both cases you agree on thinking on risk in terms of random losses. Differences arise when quantifying risk in practice, because usually an actuary works with random variables in which positive values identify losses and, therefore, she is worried about what happens in the right tail of the distributions. Nonetheless, a practitioner from the financial industry usually works with random variables where positive values identify gains or profits, so she is mainly worried about the behavior of the left tail of the distributions. Therefore, depending on where you come from, you would be used to look at risk quantification from different perspectives. More precisely, we should talk about 'liability side' practitioners and 'asset side' practitioners instead of 'insurance' and 'financial' practitioners. For instance, an example of financial practitioners that take (what we have called) a 'liability side' perspective when quantifying risk are those in charge of assessing credit risk. On the other side, as we will discuss later, the perspective used in European insurance regulation to quantify solvency capital requirements is an 'asset side' perspective and not a 'liability side' perspective (as it could be expected because of the nature of this industry's business).

Although moving from one perspective to the other is not a big issue, few guidelines to reach this goal are outlined. It is our opinion that these are the kind of helpful indications that bridge the gap between theory and practice, and between insurance ('liability side') and financial ('asset side') practitioners. The following guidelines are summarized in Table 1.4, in order to provide a fast and visual reference when needed.

Table 1.4   Risk quantification: 'liability side' versus 'asset side' perspectives

Concept	Liability side perspective	Asset side perspective
Notation for risk measures used in this Table	ρ	r
Target random variable	X a random loss	X a random profit
Monotonicity	$P(X_1 \leqslant X_2) = 1 \Rightarrow$ $\rho(X_1) \leqslant \rho(X_2)$	$P(X_1 \leqslant X_2) = 1 \Rightarrow$ $\mathrm{r}(X_1) \geqslant \mathrm{r}(X_2)$
	From the liability side perspective, smaller losses should have associated smaller risk measurements. On the asset side perspective, the higher the gain the lesser its risk value.	
Translation invariance	$\rho(X + c) = \rho(X) + c,$ $\forall\, c \in \mathbb{R}$	$\mathrm{r}(X + c) = \mathrm{r}(X) - c,$ $\forall\, c \in \mathbb{R}$

Continued on next page

Table 1.4: continued from previous page

Concept	Liability side perspective	Asset side perspective
	A positive amount of money from the liability side perspective may be considered as a loss, while from the asset side perspective it is exactly the opposite. Therefore, if the risk measure satisfies the translation invariance property, a positive amount of money must increase risk from the liability side perspective while the same positive amount of money must decrease risk from the asset side perspective.	
Relevance	$X \geqslant 0$ and $X \neq 0 \Rightarrow$ $\rho(X) > 0$	$X \leqslant 0$ and $X \neq 0 \Rightarrow$ $\mathrm{r}(X) > 0$
Strictness	$\rho(X) \geqslant \mathbb{E}(X)$	$\mathrm{r}(X) \geqslant -\mathbb{E}(X)$
	Recalling that X represents a random loss from the liability side perspective and a gain from the asset side perspective.	
Subadditivity, Positive homogeneity, Comonotonic additivity, Convexity, Law invariance	Formal expressions from both perspectives remain as they are displayed in Table 1.2, except for replacing ρ by r.	

For any random variables X_1, X_2, $X \in \Gamma$.

Additional comments with respect to differences among the 'liability side' and the 'asset side' perspective for risk quantification may be found, for instance, in Rüschendorf [2013]. As an example, Definition 1.8 has been introduced from a 'liability side' perspective, so positive values of random variable X are considered losses. Considering expressions in Definition 1.8 and adopting an 'asset side' perspective, if one is interested in obtaining the VaR at α confidence level for a continuous random variable Z with positive values representing profits, then the correct risk figure would be obtained as

$$\begin{aligned} &\text{'VaR of } Z \text{ at confidence level } \alpha \in (0,1)\text{'} \\ &\qquad = -\mathrm{VaR}_{1-\alpha}(Z) \text{ following Definition 1.8.} \end{aligned} \tag{1.7}$$

The perspective taken in the following chapters of this book is the one that we have called 'liability side' perspective.

1.2.2 Some misunderstandings to be avoided in practice

Risk measures versus their estimates

It is quite frequent to confuse a risk measure with the procedures used to estimate it. These two concepts are different and their identification can lead to misunderstandings. Fortunately, the spread of knowledge about risk measurement makes these kind of doubts less frequent than they were before. But when having first contact with risk measurement (for instance, if you are an undergraduate student interested in this topic or a recently hired practitioner without previous experience in the insurance industry or the financial sector) this is one of the most common mistakes. Diagram in Figure 1.2 may help to clarify concepts.

Figure 1.2 Basic mind map for risk quantification.

$$\begin{array}{ccc} \textbf{Theory} & \xrightarrow{\text{Assumptions}} & \textbf{Practice} \\ \text{Risk measure } (\rho) & \xrightarrow{\rho \text{ To } \widehat{\rho}} & \boxed{\text{Risk figure est. } \widehat{\rho}(\widehat{X})} \\ & & \uparrow \\ \text{Random variable } (X) & \xrightarrow{X \text{ To } \widehat{X}} & \text{R.v. estimation } (\widehat{X}) \end{array} \tag{1.8}$$

Figure 1.2 is intended to depict a schematic situation faced when trying to quantify risk. On the one hand, theoretical aspects related to the risk measure (the instrument to summarize risk) and the target random variable (the source of risk) must be taken into account. These theoretical aspects are represented on the left hand side of the diagram, and should correspond to answers to questions such as the following: Is the selected risk measure adequate? Is the target random variable observable?...On the other hand, figures are basic in practice. As long as the final objective is to obtain an estimate of the incurred risk (framed box in Figure 1.2) assumptions have to be in place to move from theory to practice. So, the assumptions made to estimate both the risk measure and the target random variable become crucial. They are so relevant that, from our point of view, they can lead to the confusion that we are highlighting here. This is because, in daily practice, one could deliver risk figures estimations (right hand side of the diagram) without worrying about theoretical aspects (left hand side). As mentioned before, let us put some examples.

Example 1.2 (Historical VaR). Measuring risk in practice using the historical VaR methodology has been relatively common because it has an easy implementation. Properly speaking, it is not a unique methodology as we try to justify hereinafter. From the point of view provided by the diagram in Figure 1.2, on the theoretical side this methodology takes into account as risk measure ρ the VaR with some confidence level $\alpha \in (0, 1)$ and considers that the target random variable X is observable. Moreover, it is assumed that observations of that random variable from past periods can be obtained. The assumptions for moving from theory to practice are as follows: with respect to the estimation of the target random variable $\widehat{X}$, it is assumed that future realizations will be exactly the same as past realizations, so past observations that have been obtained are going to be considered future observations too. And with respect to the estimation $\widehat{\rho}$ of VaR, there is not a unique feasible assumption (and this is why we consider the 'historical VaR' a set of methodologies and not just one). For instance, a feasible assumption is to consider the data set of observations of $\widehat{X}$ as it represents the discrete random variable X which only takes those particular values and no more. Consequently, VaR should be estimated as the empirical α-quantile of that set. But, if the data set of observations of $\widehat{X}$ is considered just a sample of X, then any α-quantile approximation[1] of data set $\widehat{X}$ could be used to obtain the final risk figure estimation $\widehat{\rho}(\widehat{X})$ of $\rho(X)$.

Example 1.3 (Normal VaR). Bearing in mind diagram in Figure 1.2, this methodology takes as theoretical risk measure ρ the VaR at some confidence level $\alpha \in (0, 1)$, and considers as target random variable X one which is assumed to be normally distributed. Assumptions to move from the theoretical side to the practical one are as follows: with respect to X, it is assumed

---

[1] For instance, quantile function in software R has more than 10 different ways to approximate the α-quantile, where the one coded by 0 is what we have called the empirical quantile. Even MS Excel has implemented functions INC.PERCENTILE and EXC.PERCENTILE which return different approximations of the α-quantile.

that $X \sim N(\mu, \sigma^2)$ for some $\mu \in \mathbb{R}$ and $\sigma > 0$, and that the practitioner is able to estimate μ and σ in some way (maybe from data or from expert judgment, for instance), so it is feasible to obtain $\hat{\mu}$ and $\hat{\sigma}$ estimates of μ and σ, respectively. With respect to the risk measure, the assumption made on the random variable implicitly provides a closed-form expression for VaR, because if $X \sim N(\mu, \sigma^2)$ then $\text{VaR}_\alpha(X) = \mu + \sigma \cdot q_\alpha$, where q_α is the α-quantile of a standard normal distribution (as it has been shown in Table 1.3). As it happened with the historical VaR methodology, the Normal VaR methodology may be understood as a set of methodologies depending on the particular chosen way for estimating the parameters of the distribution. In the end, $\rho(X)$ is estimated by $\hat{\mu} + \hat{\sigma} \cdot q_\alpha$.

Note that the Normal VaR methodology is frequently used for sums of normally distributed random variables. On the theoretical side, if $n > 1$ random variables $X_i \sim N(\mu_i, \sigma_i^2)$, $i = 1, \ldots, n$, are considered and $\Lambda = (\rho_{ij})_{i,j \in \{1,\ldots,n\}}$ is the correlation matrix for pairs of those random variables, then it is known that

$$X = \sum_{i=1}^{n} X_i \sim N\left(\sum_{i=1}^{n} \mu_i, \sigma^2\right),$$

where $\sigma^2 = \vec{\mu}' \cdot \Lambda \cdot \vec{\mu}$ and $\vec{\mu}$ is an n-dimensional vector whose components are μ_i, $i = 1, \ldots, n$. So, the situation is just the one described in the previous paragraph, taking as $\mu = \sum_{i=1}^{n} \mu_i$ and as $\sigma = \sqrt{\vec{\mu}' \cdot \Lambda \cdot \vec{\mu}}$. In this case, the process to obtain parameter estimates $\hat{\mu}$ and $\hat{\sigma}$ must take into account that correlation coefficients ρ_{ij} should also be estimated. In other words,

$$\hat{\sigma} = \sqrt{\hat{\vec{\mu}}' \cdot \hat{\Lambda} \cdot \hat{\vec{\mu}}}.$$

Example 1.4 (Cornish-Fisher VaR). As in the previous examples, different methodologies are embraced under this name. They share the following elements: on the one hand, the theoretical risk measure ρ is the VaR with some confidence level $\alpha \in (0, 1)$ and no hypothesis about the distribution function of the target random variable is made. Nonetheless, it is assumed that some higher order moments of X exist and are finite. On the other hand, assumptions for moving from the theoretical side to the practical side are that, in order to obtain an estimation $\hat{\rho}(\hat{X})$, a closed-form approximation similar to the one valid for normally distributed random variables is achievable. For that purpose, modified α-quantiles are devised taking into account estimations of finite order moments of X. Differences between Cornish-Fisher VaR methodologies come from the maximum order of moments considered in the quantile estimations. For instance, in Chapter 4 we have used third order Cornish-Fisher VaR approximations, but is is usual to find fourth order Cornish-Fisher VaR approximations in financial applications.

VaR versus Mean-VaR

An apparently harmless sentence like 'most financial credit risk models used in practice to quantify risk are based on VaR at some confidence level', which most practitioners and researchers in this field may subscribe, can have undesired consequences if it is misunderstood. The main concern with the previous sentence is that nothing is said about the random variable to which the VaR is applied to: even considering the same confidence level and the same input data, different figures can be obtained depending on the underlying random variable under inspection. For instance, a large number of banks use internal models to simulate losses generated by credit events affecting their loans. Let us focus on one bank and let us denote its aggregate simulated losses by X. Therefore, the amount of money needed to cover unexpected losses (its *economic capital*) is probably computed as

$$EC = \text{VaR}_{99.9\%}(X - \mathbb{E}(X))$$

in order to take into account its simulated values and also regulatory requirements (Basel II/III). Note that in this case, although the random variable simulated is X, the one used to quantify risk (i.e., to obtain the economic capital) is $U = X - \mathbb{E}(X)$, in fact. The VaR is a risk measure that satisfies the translation invariance property shown in Table 1.2 and, therefore,

$$EC = \text{VaR}_{99.9\%}(U) = \text{VaR}_{99.9\%}(X) - \mathbb{E}(X). \tag{1.9}$$

This last expression for the EC is certainly more familiar to financial practitioners. Moreover, sometimes $\rho(X) = \text{VaR}_{99.9\%}(X) - \mathbb{E}(X)$ is considered the value that another risk measure ρ named 'Mean Value at Risk'(Mean-VaR) returns when applied to random loss X. Expression (1.9) has been intentionally displayed in second place in order to stress the following idea. Let us imagine now an European insurance company calculating its Solvency Capital Requirement (SCR) under the Solvency II regulatory framework and by using an internal model. Let us suppose that within the model a set of stochastic basic own funds of the company for the next year is simulated. In such a case, if Y denotes the 'basic own funds for the next year' random variable, then taking into account expression (1.7) it seems reasonable that the following expression

$$SCR = \text{VaR}_{99.5\%}(-Y) = -\text{VaR}_{0.5\%}(Y) \tag{1.10}$$

would be used to compute the SCR, because it perfectly fits the regulatory requirements[2]. But what it is relevant here is that it makes no sense to require the company to set aside, as a cushion against insolvency, the following amount of money

$$\text{SCR} = \text{VaR}_{99.5\%}(-Y) - \mathbb{E}(-Y) = \text{VaR}_{99.5\%}(-Y) + \mathbb{E}(Y). \quad (1.11)$$

Due to misunderstanding of expression (1.9) for the EC, and transposing it for the SCR expression simply replacing X by $-Y$, figures with non economic sense are attained. Why? Basically because X and $-Y$ are essentially different. Random variable X is a pure loss while $-Y$ contains both losses and gains. In fact, hopefully $\mathbb{E}(-Y) \ll 0$ (the insurance company expects substantial gains) and reasonably $\mathbb{E}(X) > 0$ (the expectation of a set of losses is also a loss). In words, when computing the EC the focus is set on random variable $U = X - \mathbb{E}(X)$ because it is assumed that the quantity $\mathbb{E}(X)$ is already accounted for on the liability side of the balance sheet (which is not entirely simulated by the credit risk model) to mitigate credit losses. On the other hand, the model for the SCR of the insurance company is simulating the whole balance sheet. Therefore $-Y$ is not comparable with X because losses associated to $-Y$ are those that have exceeded all the mitigation tools and strategies that the company has in place, while X losses are computed gross of any mitigation effect.

Example 1.5. A toy example can help us to illustrate the impact of such a misunderstanding. Imagine two insurance companies c_1 and c_2, one with $Y_{1,t} = 100$ monetary units (m.u.) of present basic own funds and the other with $Y_{2,t} = 1$ m.u. Both use the same model to project next year basic own funds (let us say $Y_{1,t+1}$ and $Y_{2,t+1}$) and the same methodology to compute VaR at the 99.5% confidence level. To simplify things, let us assume that $\mathbb{E}(Y_{i,t+1}) = Y_{i,t}$ for $i = 1, 2$, so the expectation of projected basic owns funds for the next year is nothing but the value of the actual basic own funds of each company. Imagine that the risk figures that these companies obtain are $\text{VaR}_{99.5\%}(-Y_{1,t+1}) = 5$ and $\text{VaR}_{99.5\%}(-Y_{2,t+1}) = 0.5$. They may be interpreted in the following way: c_1 is going to suffer a minimum loss of a 5% of its present basic own funds in a 0.5% of the future scenarios considered, while c_2 is going to suffer a minimum loss of a 50% of its present basic own funds in a 0.5% of the future scenarios considered. Interpreted in that way,

---

[2] As it is shown with this expression, the core of the European insurance regulation uses what we have called an 'asset side' perspective when talking about risk quantification.

c_2 seems highly riskier than c_1. And this would properly be reflected using expression (1.10), because their respective solvency capital requirements will be $SCR(c_1) = 5$ m.u. and $SCR(c_2) = 0.5$ m.u. which, in terms of their present basic own funds, represent reasonable risk proportions. But note that if misunderstandings are in place and expression (1.11) is used instead of expression (1.10) to compute their SCR, then $SCR(c_1) = 5 + 100 = 105$ m.u. and $SCR(c_2) = 0.5 + 1 = 1.5$ m.u. are obtained. These figures are far from representing neither the risk faced by the companies nor their relative riskiness.

Somebody could think that the previous examples overweight the importance of items on the right hand side of Figure 1.2. These examples have been chosen because they correspond to common risk quantification issues found in practice and researchers must bear them in mind. Nevertheless, it is also our intention to aware that practitioners should spend some time on thinking of questions related to the left hand side of that Figure, this is, on theoretical aspects related to a practical risk quantification in a regular basis. Some of these questions are listed below, although it is neither an extensive list nor a prioritized one:

· Have several risk measures been considered before the final selection is made?

· Do these risk measures satisfy properties that we consider necessary?

· Are these risk measures or their confidence levels regulatory driven?

· Have we an idea about the implicit risk attitude behind using those particular risk measures?

· What are we looking for as the final result of this risk quantification process?

· Are we aware about our capability (in terms of time, resources and knowledge) to transform ideas into numbers? In other words, for every considered risk measure and every target random variable, do we know how to move from the theoretical side to the practical side?

· Have we properly defined our target random variable?

· Does the target random variable depend on other random variables easier to measure or identify?

· How precise do we need to be in our estimations?

Hopefully, useful ideas about how to answer some of these question may be found in this book or in the references therein. We would like to close this chapter with some last remarks. As it has already been said, main references used to build this chapter are books Denuit *et al.* [2005] and Rüschendorf [2013]. Note that the CTE risk measure introduced in Definition 1.10 is called Expected Shortfall (ES) in McNeil *et al.* [2005] and, therefore, there is also a difference with the Definition 1.12 of ES provided in this book. Moreover, names for several risk measures in Section 1.1 do not match the ones used for equivalent risk measures in Rüschendorf [2013]. This remark makes evident that there is yet no common consensus in risk measures naming.

For an interesting way to study basic risk measures but without a parametric model assumption, the work by Alemany *et al.* [2013] shows how to implement kernel estimation of the probability density function and how to derive the risk measure from there. Kernel estimation is specially useful when the number of observations is large. Bolancé *et al.* [2003]; Buch-Larsen *et al.* [2005]; Bolancé *et al.* [2008] explain how to address heavy-tailed or skewed distributions. The interested reader can find several contributions using other models and non-parametric approaches in Bolance *et al.* [2008]; Guillen *et al.* [2011, 2013]. Bolancé *et al.* [2012, 2013] provide data-driven examples with R and SAS code in the context of operational risk problems. Multivariate risk quantification is addressed by Bolancé *et al.* [2014]; Bahraoui *et al.* [2014].

With respect to a deeper analysis of issues of Solvency II for practitioners and regarding theoretical aspects behind Cornish-Fisher expansions, the interested reader is referred to Sandström [2011]. Last but not least, one topic not covered by this book that has to be taken into account in risk quantification is the model risk. Aggarwal *et al.* [2016] provides a wide variety of approaches to deal with this real challenge and may be an interesting departure point to anyone interested in this topic.

1.3   Exercises

1. Consider the following empirical distribution

$$13, \ 15, \ 26, \ 26, \ 26, \ 37, \ 37, \ 100$$

Determine the $\text{VaR}_{85\%}(X)$ and $\text{TVaR}_{85\%}(X)$.

2. Consider the following distribution function $F(x) = \dfrac{x^2}{9}$ for $0 < x \leqslant 3$. Find the $\text{VaR}_{85\%}(X)$ and $\text{TVaR}_{85\%}(X)$.

3. Given that

$$\mathrm{VaR}_{90\%}(X) = 50, \quad \mathrm{ES}_{90\%}(X) = 13 \quad \text{and} \quad \mathrm{CVaR}_{90\%}(X) = 260.$$

a) Calculate $\mathrm{TVaR}_{90\%}(X)$, $S_X(\mathrm{VaR}_{90\%}(X))$ and $\mathrm{CTE}_{90\%}(X)$.

b) Discuss if it is possible that loss X would be an absolutely continuous random variable.

4. Show that the TVaR of a random variable X distributed by the Normal distribution $\mathcal{N}(\mu, \sigma^2)$ is equal to $\mathrm{TVaR}_\alpha = \mu + \sigma \cdot \dfrac{\phi(\Phi^{-1}(\alpha))}{1 - \alpha}$, where ϕ and Φ^{-1} stand for the standard Normal pdf and quantile function, respectively.

a) Demonstrate that the properties of *Translation invariance*, *Positive homogeneity* and *Strictness* are satisfied in this case.

b) Repeat the exercise for the CVaR_α.

5. Analyze if the properties of *Translation invariance*, *Positive homogeneity* and *Strictness* are satisfied by the VaR and TVaR when:

a) the random variable X is distributed by the Lognormal distribution $\mathcal{LN}(\mu, \sigma^2)$.

b) the random variable X is distributed by the Generalized Pareto distribution $\mathcal{GPD}(0, \sigma)$.

2 Data on losses for risk evaluation

Historical loss data is of key importance for risk management and modeling of losses. This statistical information must be carefully analyzed and understood in order to extract the best possible knowledge. Therefore, it is important to collect details on the data sources, such as framework, time of collection, definitions, exceptions and so on.

Insurance companies have always been collecting data for risk management purposes, but in the past information was rather aggregate whereas nowadays, there is much more detailed knowledge on individual policy holders, events, claims handling and loss compensations. Nevertheless, data quality still remains a challenge for many insurers and the lack of robustness of statistical information may sometimes pose huge problems to the undertaking of ambitious risk management initiatives.

This chapter presents examples of loss data, which are used throughout some parts of this book. They are intended to be helpful to understand concepts. They do not intend to represent any particular insurance company.

Thereafter, we continue by discussing several characteristics of the loss severity information that has been specially created for this book and their aggregation by means of their sum. This analysis involves statistical description in this chapter and, in the following chapters, we address the implementation of risk measurement and capital allocation. Having a good understanding of amounts of losses is important not only for modeling purposes, but also to identify effective management and mitigating actions.

2.1 An example on three dimensional data

Historical loss information is the main source of knowledge for the specific experience and history of the organization. Sources of information on loss events that occurred in comparable companies can sometimes be helpful to understand their position with respect to exposure and their corresponding risk. It is sometimes also useful to compare lines of business or business units within a single company.

Throughout most chapters of this book the same data set will be examined. The data consist of three sources of loss and the sum of them. We make use of an artificial sample to provide with a guided path to implementation. Because of the loss amounts have been artificially generated they do not have monetary dimension other than 'monetary units'. Nevertheless, in several parts of the book we consider that these loss amounts are the cost of claims in thousands of euros for three types of damage, let us say *property damage*, *bodily injuries* and *medical expenses*. Table 2.1 and Table 2.2 show some statistical characteristics of the sample, and Figure 2.1 presents a visual view of the three variables and their sum.

There are some interesting features about the example data that are presented in this chapter. All the variables are asymmetric with a few large values and many small values. The maximum values for both X_1 and X_2 are much higher than the average. The minimum values are always strictly positive. We also note that the minimum of the sum is not the sum of the minimum and this is due to the fact that the data are paired, and the minimum of each marginal does not necessarily correspond to the minimum observed value of the other marginal.

When comparing the data on Figure 2.1, we note that the size of the losses and the shape of the histograms are similar between sources X_1 and X_2 but not between them and source X_3. Additionally, we cannot see the dependence patterns between the sources unless we look into the bivariate plots. The joint behavior is presented in Figure 2.2.

Table 2.1   Statistical summary of the example loss data

Data	Mean	Median	Std. Deviation	Maximum
X_1	0.707	0.033	3.778	49.812
X_2	0.450	0.033	3.369	52.129
X_3	0.268	0.105	0.361	1.775
$X_1 + X_2 + X_3$	1.426	0.221	5.6797	103.716

There are 350 losses for each variable

Table 2.2   Statistical summary of the example loss data (part II)

Data	Minimum	Variance	Skewness	Kurtosis
X_1	0.001	14.273	8.875	94.353
X_2	0.001	11.350	12.401	171.107
X_3	0.003	0.130	2.119	4.296
$X_1 + X_2 + X_3$	0.026	46.199	11.354	153.368

There are 350 losses for each variable

Figure 2.1   Histograms of loss data originating from sources X_1, X_2, X_3 and their sum

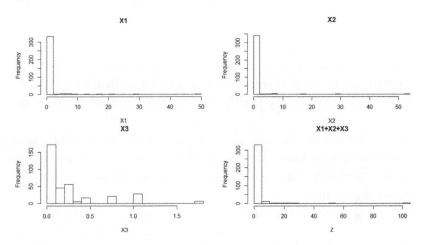

2.2   Basic graphical analysis of the loss severity distributions

We can measure risk because different outcomes occur with different probabilities. Loss Distribution Analysis (LDA) is a method used to calculate and evaluate the risk that is induced by losses that occur randomly. Historical data can be helpful to predict future behavior, and so it is important to analyze its density shape.

Modeling the severity of losses usually involves analysis of parametric distributions such as the Normal distribution and all other distributions that

Figure 2.2   Dependence from sources X_1, X_2, X_3 and their sum

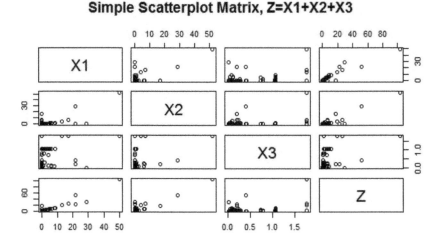

have been mentioned in the previous chapter. However, it is very difficult to find a parametric distribution that fits all sizes of loss: (i) low severities occur frequently, (ii) high severities occur much less often, and (iii) catastrophic losses only occur very rarely. They are usually referred as rare losses or rare events.

This section presents the analysis of one parametric distribution that can be used to fit the behavior observed in the sample data. Some other basic parametric distributions for severity not considered here were presented in the previous chapter.

We have estimated the Normal densities using maximum likelihood in all variables, X_1, X_2, X_3 and the sum of the three. Some results are shown in Figures 2.3 to 2.5. In there, we present the parametric Normal pdf estimate and the original data, the former appearing as dashed lines. On the left, the plots show the lower values of the observed sample and on the right the higher observed values are presented. Low and high values are split in order to see the parts of the densities where data are scarce. Only a simple parametric density estimate is presented in this chapter, but practitioners often use more sophisticated distributions. The empirical distribution function obtained for the sample data is also a possibility, and in this case it is not necessary to fit any distribution in particular.

Figures 2.3 to 2.5 show the maximum likelihood estimation of the Normal densities for the data. The right hand side tail is presented. The density may still be too low for large losses.

Figure 2.3   The estimated density for the X_1 data using the Normal distribution

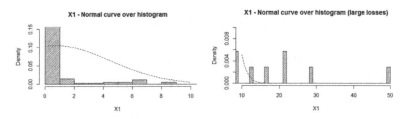

Figure 2.4   The estimated density for the X_2 data using the Normal distribution

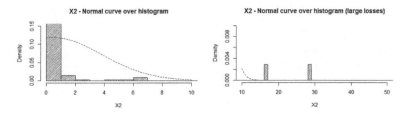

Figure 2.5   The estimated density for the X_3 data using the Normal distribution

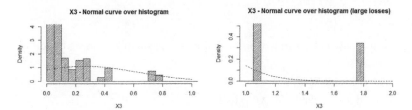

2.3   Quantile estimation

Quantile estimation for the parametric distribution presented in the previous section, other distributions or the empirical distribution functions can be performed using the inverse of the distribution function evaluated at the maximum likelihood parameter estimates. This is one of the most basic risk assessment tools that will be used throughout this book and, if one think about Figure 1.2, this is the sort of tools necessary to move from theory to practice.

2.4   Examples

Illustrative examples of quantitative analysis are developed in the programming language R. The dataset used in this Chapter (*exampleERM*) is available at `http://www.ub.edu/rfa/ERM`.

1. Download and save the data in an appropriate directory. Prepare the data:
   ```
   example < − read.table("exampleERM.txt",header=TRUE)
   riskloss < − as.matrix(example)
   ```

2. Descriptive analysis in R. The number of observations and a set of descriptives can be computed as follows:
   ```
   n < − nrow(riskloss)
   summary(riskloss)
   E.di < − colMeans(val.di)
   Cov.di < − var(val.di)

   library(moments)
    skewness(riskloss[ ,"X1"])
    kurtosis(riskloss[ ,"X1"])
   ```

3. Graphical analysis in R. Compute the histogram of X1 and scatterplots as follows:
   ```
   hist(riskloss[,"X1"], 20)
   lines(density(riskloss[,"X1"])),lwd=3)

   plot(riskloss[ ,"X1"], type="l", ylim=c(0,10))
   lines(riskloss[ ,"X2"], lty=2)
   lines(riskloss[ ,"X3"], lty=3)
   ```

4. Compute the $\text{VaR}_{90\%}(X1)$ and $\text{CTE}_{90\%}(X1)$
   ```
   risk1 < − riskloss[,1]
   Erisk1 < − mean(risk1)
   Vrisk1 < − var(risk1)

   VaR90 < − quantile(risk1,0.90)
    CTE90 < − mean(risk1[risk1>VaR90])
   ```

3 A family of distortion risk measures

Value at Risk (VaR) has been adopted as a standard tool to assess the risk and to calculate capital requirements in the insurance industry. As it has been shown in Chapter 1, VaR at level α is the α-quantile of a random variable X (which is often called loss). Recalling Definition 1.8

$$\text{VaR}_\alpha(X) = \inf\{x \mid F_X(x) \geq \alpha\} = F_X^{-1}(\alpha),$$

where F_X is the cumulative distribution function (cdf) of X and α is the confidence or the tolerance level $0 \leq \alpha \leq 1$. However, VaR is known to present a number of pitfalls when applied in practice. A disadvantage when using VaR in the insurance or financial contexts is that the capital requirements for catastrophic losses based on this measure can be underestimated, i.e. the necessary reserves in adverse scenarios may well be less than they should be. The underestimation of capital requirements may be aggravated when fat-tailed losses are incorrectly modeled by mild-tailed distributions, such as the Normal distribution. There are attempts to overcome this kind of model risk when using VaR or, at least, to quantify the risk related to the modelling [Alexander and Sarabia, 2012]. But, in addition, a second drawback is that the VaR may fail the subadditivity property. As it has been shown in Table 1.2 of Chapter 1, a risk measure is subadditive when the aggregated risk is less than or equal to the sum of individual risks. Subadditvity is an appealing property when aggregating risks in order to preserve the benefits of diversification. VaR is subadditive for elliptically distributed losses [McNeil *et al.*, 2005]. However, the subadditivity of VaR is not granted, as indicated in Artzner *et al.* [1999] and Acerbi and Tasche [2002].

Remember now Definition 1.9 from Chapter 1. In there Tail Value at Risk (TVaR) has been defined as

$$\text{TVaR}_\alpha(X) = \frac{1}{1-\alpha} \int_\alpha^1 \text{VaR}_\lambda(X) d\lambda.$$

Table 3.1   VaR$_{95\%}$ and TVaR$_{95\%}$ illustration

	VaR$_{95\%}$	TVaR$_{95\%}$
Empirical	47.6	125.5
Normal	87.0	105.9
Lognormal	48.9	119.1

* Cost of claims in thousands of Euro

Roughly speaking, the TVaR is understood as the mathematical expectation beyond VaR. The TVaR risk measure does not suffer the two drawbacks discussed above for VaR and, as such, would appear to be a more powerful measure for assessing the actual risks faced by insurance companies and financial institutions. However, TVaR has not been widely accepted by practitioners in the financial and insurance industry. VaR is currently the risk measure contemplated in the European solvency regulation for the insurance sector (Solvency II), and this is also the case of solvency regulation for the banking sector (Basel accords[1]). The TVaR measures average losses in the most adverse cases rather than just the minimum adverse loss, as the VaR does. Therefore, capital reserves based on the TVaR have to be considerably higher than those based on VaR and significant differences in the size of capital reserves can be obtained depending on which risk measure is adopted.

An illustration of the risk value obtained for the VaR$_{95\%}$ and TVaR$_{95\%}$ considering three alternative distributions is provided in Table 3.1. Note that huge differences in risk amounts can be obtained.

This chapter is motivated by the following question. Can a risk measure be devised that would provide a risk assessment that lies somewhere between those offered by the VaR and the TVaR? To this end, a new family of risk measures (GlueVaR) is proposed, which forms part of a wider class referred to as distortion risk measures.

GlueVaR risk measures are defined by means of a four-parameter function. By calibrating the parameters, GlueVaR risk measures can be matched to a wide variety of contexts. Specifically, once a confidence level has been fixed, the new family contains risk measures that lie between those of VaR and

---

[1] Although it seems that changing VaR by TVaR with a lower confidence level is something that is really under consideration for regulatory capital requirements in the Banking sector.

TVaR and which may adequately reflect the risk of mild-tailed distributed losses without having to resort to VaR. In certain situations, however, even more conservative risk measures than TVaR may be preferred. It is shown that these highly conservative risk measures can also be defined by means of the GlueVaR family. In order to preserve the benefits of diversification when aggregating risks, subadditivity is an appealing property of a risk measure. As it has been shown in Chapter 1, the subadditivity property ensures that the risk measure value of the aggregated risk is lower than or equal to the sum of individual risk measure values. In this chapter the subadditivity property of GlueVaR risk measures is investigated.

3.1   Overview on risk measures

Two main groups of axiom-based risk measures are *coherent risk measures*, as stated by Artzner *et al.* [1999], and *distortion risk measures*, as introduced by Wang [1996]. Concavity of the distortion function is the key element to define risk measures that belong to both groups [Wang and Dhaene, 1998]. Suggestions on new desirable properties for distortion risk measures are proposed in Balbás *et al.* [2009], while generalizations of this kind of risk measures can be found, among others, in Hürlimann [2006] and Wu and Zhou [2006]. As shown in Goovaerts *et al.* [2012], it is possible to link distortion risk measures with other interesting families of risk measures developed in the literature.

The axiomatic setting for risk measures has extensively been developed since seminal papers on coherent risk measures and distortion risk measures. Each set of axioms for risk measures corresponds to a particular behavior of decision makers under risk, as it has been shown, for instance, in Bleichrodt and Eeckhoudt [2006] and Denuit *et al.* [2006]. Most often, articles on axiom-based risk measurement present the link to a theoretical foundation of human behavior explicitly. For example, Wang [1996] shows the connection between distortion risk measures and Yaari's dual theory of choice under risk; Goovaerts *et al.* [2010] investigate the additivity of risk measures in Quiggin's rank-dependent utility theory; and Kaluszka and Krzeszowiec [2012] introduce the generalized Choquet integral premium principle and relate it to Kahneman and Tversky's cumulative prospect theory.

Many articles have appeared in recent years that pay attention to risk measures based on distortion functions or on generalizations of the quantiles. An example of the first group is Zhu and Li [2012]. Bellini and Gianin [2012] and Bellini *et al.* [2014] fit to second group. An interplay between both groups is found in Dhaene *et al.* [2012a] and Goovaerts *et al.* [2012].

3.2 Distortion risk measures

Distortion risk measures were introduced by Wang [Wang, 1995, 1996] and they are closely related to the distortion expectation theory [Yaari, 1987]. A review on how risk measures can be interpreted from several perspectives is provided in Tsanakas and Desli [2005], and a clarifying explanation of the relationship between distortion risk measures and distortion expectation theory is included. A detailed literature review of distortion risk measures is available in [Denuit *et al.*, 2005; Balbás *et al.*, 2009]. There are two key elements to define a distortion risk measure: first, the associated distortion function; and, second, the concept of the Choquet [Choquet, 1954] Integral. The distortion function, Choquet Integral and the distortion risk measure concepts can be defined as follows:

· **Distortion function.** Let $g : [0,1] \to [0,1]$ be a function such that $g(0) = 0$, $g(1) = 1$ and g is injective and non-decreasing. Then g is called a distortion function.

· **Choquet Integral.** The (asymmetric) Choquet Integral with respect to a set function μ of a μ-measurable function $X : \Omega \to \overline{\mathbb{R}}$ is denoted as $\int X d\mu$ and is equal to

$$\int X d\mu = \int_{-\infty}^{0} \left[S_{\mu,X}(x) - \mu(\Omega) \right] dx + \int_{0}^{+\infty} S_{\mu,X}(x) dx,$$

if $\mu(\Omega) < \infty$, where $S_{\mu,X}(x) = \mu(\{X > x\})$ denotes the *survival function* of X with respect to μ. Note that Ω denotes a set, which in financial and insurance applications is the sample space of a probability space. A set function μ in this context is a function defined from 2^{Ω} (the set of all subsets of Ω) to $\overline{\mathbb{R}}$. A μ-measurable function X is, widely speaking, a function defined on Ω such that expressions like $\mu(\{X > x\})$ or $\mu(\{X \leqslant x\})$ make sense. See Denneberg [1994] for more details.

· **Distortion risk measure.** Let g be a distortion function. Consider a random variable X and its survival function $S_X(x) = P(X > x)$. Then, function ρ_g defined by $\rho_g(X) = \int_{-\infty}^{0} \left[g(S_X(x)) - 1 \right] dx + \int_{0}^{+\infty} g(S_X(x)) dx$ is called a distortion risk measure.

From the previous definitions, it is straightforward to see that for any random variable X, $\rho_g(X)$ is the Choquet Integral of X with respect to the set function $\mu = g \circ P$, where P is the probability function associated with the probability space in which X is defined.

The mathematical expectation is a distortion risk measure whose distortion function is the identity function [Denuit *et al.*, 2005], this is, $\rho_{id}(X) = \mathbb{E}(X)$. Therefore, a straightforward way to interpret a distortion risk measure is as follows: first, the survival function of the random variable is distorted $(g \circ S_X)$; second, the mathematical expectation of the random variable with respect to this distorted probability is computed. From a theoretical point of view, note that this interpretation fits the discussion that risk may be defined as an expected value in many situations [Aven, 2012].

VaR and TVaR measures are in fact distortion risk measures. The associated distortion functions of these risk measures are shown in Table 3.2.

Table 3.2   VaR and TVaR distortion functions

Risk measure	Distortion function
VaR	$\psi_\alpha(u) = \begin{cases} 0 & \text{if } 0 \leqslant u < 1-\alpha \\ 1 & \text{if } 1-\alpha \leqslant u \leqslant 1, \end{cases}$
TVaR	$\gamma_\alpha(u) = \begin{cases} \dfrac{u}{1-\alpha} & \text{if } 0 \leqslant u < 1-\alpha \\ 1 & \text{if } 1-\alpha \leqslant u \leqslant 1 \end{cases}$

For a confidence level $\alpha \in (0,1)$.

Based on the distortion functions shown in Table 3.2, once α is fixed it can be proved that $\text{VaR}_\alpha(X) \leqslant \text{TVaR}_\alpha(X)$ for any random variable X.

Remark 3.1. Let g and g^* be two distortion functions and let ρ_g and ρ_{g^*} be their respective distortion risk measures. Suppose that $g(u) \leqslant g^*(u)$ for all $u \in [0,1]$. Then $\rho_g(X) \leqslant \rho_{g^*}(X)$ for any random variable X.

This result follows immediately from the definition of distortion risk measures, because

$$\rho_g(X) = \int_{-\infty}^{0} [g(S_X(x)) - 1] dx + \int_{0}^{+\infty} g(S_X(x)) dx$$
$$\leqslant \int_{-\infty}^{0} [g^*(S_X(x)) - 1] dx + \int_{0}^{+\infty} g^*(S_X(x)) dx$$
$$= \rho_{g^*}(X).$$

Many articles have recently examined risk measures based on either distortion functions [Zhu and Li, 2012; Belles-Sampera *et al.*, 2013a, 2014a, 2016b; Guillen *et al.*, 2016; Tsanakas and Millossovich, 2016] or generalizations of the quantiles [Bellini and Gianin, 2012; Bellini *et al.*, 2014]. The interplay between both of these two groups of risk measures has been examined [Dhaene *et al.*, 2012a; Goovaerts *et al.*, 2012].

3.3   A new family of risk measures: GlueVaR

A new family of distortion risk measures, named GlueVaR, is here defined. Originally, we introduced this family in Belles-Sampera *et al.* [2014a]. The main reason for defining these GlueVaR risk measures is a response to the concerns expressed by risk managers regarding the choice of risk measures in the case of regulatory capital requirements. However, as it has been already mentioned, an axiomatic approach to define or represent risk measures is more frequent in the literature [Artzner *et al.*, 1999; Föllmer and Schied, 2002; Frittelli and Rosazza Gianin, 2002; Denuit *et al.*, 2006; Song and Yan, 2009; Cerreia-Vioglio *et al.*, 2011; Ekeland *et al.*, 2012; Goovaerts *et al.*, 2012; Grechuk *et al.*, 2012].

Any GlueVaR risk measure can be described by means of its distortion function. Given a confidence level α, the distortion function for GlueVaR is:

$$\kappa_{\beta,\alpha}^{h_1,h_2}(u) = \begin{cases} \dfrac{h_1}{1-\beta} \cdot u & \text{if } 0 \leq u < 1-\beta \\ h_1 + \dfrac{h_2-h_1}{\beta-\alpha} \cdot [u-(1-\beta)] & \text{if } 1-\beta \leq u < 1-\alpha \\ 1 & \text{if } 1-\alpha \leq u \leq 1 \end{cases} \quad (3.1)$$

where $\alpha, \beta \in [0,1]$ such that $\alpha \leq \beta$, $h_1 \in [0,1]$ and $h_2 \in [h_1,1]$. Parameter β is the additional confidence level besides α. The shape of the GlueVaR distortion function is determined by the distorted survival probabilities h_1 and h_2 at levels $1-\beta$ and $1-\alpha$, respectively. We call parameters h_1 and h_2 the heights of the distortion function.

A wide range of risk measures may be defined under this framework. Note that VaR_α and TVaR_α are particular cases of this new family of risk measures. Namely, VaR_α and TVaR_α correspond to distortion functions $\kappa_{\alpha,\alpha}^{0,0}$ and $\kappa_{\alpha,\alpha}^{1,1}$, respectively. By establishing suitable conditions on the heights h_1 and h_2, the GlueVaR family is very flexible. For example, risk managers might like to select α, β, h_1 and h_2 so that

$$\text{VaR}_\alpha(X) \leq \text{GlueVaR}_{\beta,\alpha}^{h_1,h_2}(X) \leq \text{TVaR}_\alpha(X).$$

This can be achieved by selecting a set of parameters for their associated distortion functions to ensure that $\psi_\alpha(u) \leq \kappa_{\beta,\alpha}^{h_1,h_2}(u) \leq \gamma_\alpha(u)$ for any $u \in [0,1]$, following remark 3.1, i.e. by forcing condition $h_1 \leq \dfrac{1-\beta}{1-\alpha}$. An example of such a case is shown in Figure 3.1 (left-hand side).

The GlueVaR family also allows us to define a highly conservative risk measure GlueVaR$_{\beta,\alpha}^{h_1,h_2}$, such that

$$\text{TVaR}_\alpha(X) \leq \text{GlueVaR}_{\beta,\alpha}^{h_1,h_2}(X) \leq \text{TVaR}_\beta(X)$$

for any X and that the associated distortion function $\kappa_{\beta,\alpha}^{h_1,h_2}$ is concave in $[0,1]$. In this case, $\dfrac{1-\beta}{1-\alpha} \leq h_1$ and $h_2 = 1$ must be fulfilled, as occurs in the example shown in Figure 3.1 (right-hand side).

Figure 3.1   Examples of GlueVaR distortion functions.
Left. Distortion function is concave in $[0, 1-\alpha)$ and VaR$_\alpha(X) \leq$ GlueVaR$_{\beta,\alpha}^{h_1,h_2}(X) \leq$ TVaR$_\alpha(X)$ for a random variable X;
Right. Distortion function is concave in the whole range $[0,1]$ and TVaR$_\alpha(X) \leq$ GlueVaR$_{\beta,\alpha}^{h_1,h_2}(X) \leq$ TVaR$_\beta(X)$ for a random variable X.

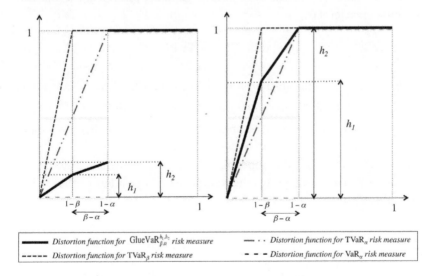

——— Distortion function for GlueVaR$_{\beta,\alpha}^{h_1,h_2}$ risk measure	— · · Distortion function for TVaR$_\alpha$ risk measure
- - - - - Distortion function for TVaR$_\beta$ risk measure	- - - Distortion function for VaR$_\alpha$ risk measure

3.4   Linear combination of risk measures

Given a random variable X and for fixed tolerance levels α and β so that $\alpha < \beta$, GlueVaR$_{\beta,\alpha}^{h_1,h_2}(X)$ can be expressed as a linear combination of TVaR$_\beta(X)$,

$\text{TVaR}_\alpha(X)$ and $\text{VaR}_\alpha(X)$. This result allows us to translate the graphical-based construction of GlueVaR risk measures into an algebraic construction based on standard risk measures.

If the following notation is used,

$$
\begin{cases}
\omega_1 = h_1 - \dfrac{(h_2 - h_1) \cdot (1 - \beta)}{\beta - \alpha} \\[2ex]
\omega_2 = \dfrac{h_2 - h_1}{\beta - \alpha} \cdot (1 - \alpha) \\[2ex]
\omega_3 = 1 - \omega_1 - \omega_2 = 1 - h_2,
\end{cases}
\tag{3.2}
$$

then the distortion function $\kappa_{\beta,\alpha}^{h_1,h_2}(u)$ in (3.1) may be rewritten as (details can be found in Section A.1 of the Appendix):

$$
\kappa_{\beta,\alpha}^{h_1,h_2}(u) = \omega_1 \cdot \gamma_\beta(u) + \omega_2 \cdot \gamma_\alpha(u) + \omega_3 \cdot \psi_\alpha(u)
\tag{3.3}
$$

where γ_β, γ_α, ψ_α are the distortion functions of TVaR at confidence levels β and α and of VaR at confidence level α, respectively (see Table 3.2). Therefore GlueVaR is a risk measure that can be expressed as a linear combination of three risk measures: TVaR at confidence levels β and α and VaR at confidence level α,

$$
\text{GlueVaR}_{\beta,\alpha}^{h_1,h_2}(X) = \omega_1 \cdot \text{TVaR}_\beta(X) + \omega_2 \cdot \text{TVaR}_\alpha(X) + \omega_3 \cdot \text{VaR}_\alpha(X).
\tag{3.4}
$$

Given this relationship, an alternative notation for $\text{GlueVaR}_{\beta,\alpha}^{h_1,h_2}(X)$ and its related distortion function can be used. The notation $\text{GlueVaR}_{\beta,\alpha}^{\omega_1,\omega_2}(X)$ or $\kappa_{\beta,\alpha}^{\omega_1,\omega_2}(u)$ may, on occasions, be preferred to that based on heights h_1 and h_2. The bijective relationship between pairs (h_1, h_2) and (ω_1, ω_2) is also shown in Section A.2 of the Appendix.

Specifically, in order to simplify the statement of Proposition 4.1, the expression of $\kappa_{\beta,\alpha}^{\omega_1,\omega_2}(u)$ is

$$
\kappa_{\beta,\alpha}^{\omega_1,\omega_2}(u) =
\begin{cases}
\left[\dfrac{\omega_1}{1-\beta} + \dfrac{\omega_2}{1-\alpha} \right] \cdot u & \text{if } 0 \leq u < 1-\beta \\[2ex]
\omega_1 + \dfrac{\omega_2}{1-\alpha} \cdot u & \text{if } 1-\beta \leq u < 1-\alpha \\[2ex]
1 & \text{if } 1-\alpha \leq u \leq 1
\end{cases}
\tag{3.5}
$$

An interesting interpretation of (3.4) in the context of decision making and risk management is that GlueVaR risk measures arise as a linear combination of three possible scenarios. So, two levels of severity tolerance can be fixed, namely α and β, with $\alpha < \beta$. Then, the risk can be measured in the highly conservative scenario with TVaR at level β; in the conservative scenario with TVaR at level α; and in the less conservative scenario with VaR at level α.

Each combination of these risk scenarios reflects a concrete risk attitude. Therefore, it can be said that the combination of these risk scenarios in this context is something that is directly identified by an explicit GlueVaR risk measure. To some extent, these risk attitudes could be related to risk appetite [Aven, 2013].

From the practitioner's point of view, four parameters must be fixed in order to define the GlueVaR risk measure. The α and β values correspond to the confidence levels used for bad and very bad scenarios, respectively. For instance, $\alpha = 95\%$ and $\beta = 99.5\%$ could be selected, which are equivalent to one bad event every twenty years or one bad event every two hundred, respectively. The other two parameters are directly related to the weights given to these scenarios. For instance, it could be said that the three components of GlueVaR in expression (3.4) are equally important. This would imply $\omega_1 = \omega_2 = \omega_3 = 1/3$, so the corresponding h_1 and h_2 parameters could be found. When $\omega_1 = \omega_2 = \omega_3 = 1/3$ and $\alpha = 95\%$, $\beta = 99.5\%$, these parameters are $h_1 = 11/30$ and $h_2 = 2/3$.

3.5   Subadditivity

In a seminal article [Artzner et al., 1999] the following set of axioms that a risk measure should satisfy was established: positive homogeneity, translation invariance, monotonicity and subadditivity. Authors referred to such risk measures as *coherent risk measures*. Distortion risk measures always satisfy the first three properties, but subadditivity is only guaranteed when the distortion function is concave [Denneberg, 1994; Wang and Dhaene, 1998; Wirch and Hardy, 2002]. Therefore, VaR, unlike TVaR, is not coherent. In some situations, coherence of risk measures is a requirement [Cox, 2012] but, nonetheless, some criticisms can be found [Dhaene et al., 2008]. Additional properties for distortion risk measures are provided in [Jiang, 2008; Balbás et al., 2009], which may complement the list of properties for risk measures shown in Tables 1.2 and 1.4 of Chapter 1. In this section we focus on the subadditivity property.

In order to preserve the benefits of diversification when aggregating risks, subadditivity is an appealing property of a risk measure. As it has been shown in Chapter 1, the subadditivity property ensures that the risk measure value of the aggregated risk is lower than or equal to the sum of individual risk measure values. For distortion risk measures, subadditivity may be defined as follows.

Definition 3.1. Given a confidence level $\alpha \in [0, 1]$, a distortion risk measure ρ_g is subadditive if, for any pair X, Y,

$$\int (X + Y) d(g \circ P) \leqslant \int X d(g \circ P) + \int Y d(g \circ P),$$

where the integral symbol stands for Choquet Integrals with respect to the set function $g \circ P$.

The Choquet integral condition used in the definition can be rewritten, in terms of survival functions and Lebesgue integrals, as

$$\int_0^{+\infty} g\left(S_{X+Y}(z)\right) dz \leqslant \int_0^{+\infty} g\left(S_X(x)\right) dx + \int_0^{+\infty} g\left(S_Y(y)\right) dy.$$

As shown, GlueVaR risk measures may be interpreted as a linear combination of VaR and TVaR risk measures. Therefore, a GlueVaR risk measure is coherent when the weight assigned to VaR is zero and the weights of the TVaR_α and TVaR_β are non-negative. In terms of the parameters of the distortion function, GlueVaR is subadditive (and thus coherent) if $h_2 = 1$ and $\dfrac{1-\beta}{1-\alpha} \leqslant h_1$. More generally, any property satisfied by TVaR but not by VaR will be inherited by GlueVaR if $\omega_1 \geqslant 0$ and $\omega_3 = 0$ in expression (3.2).

Subaddtitivity in the whole domain is a strong condition. When dealing with fat tail losses (i.e. low-frequency and large-loss events), risk managers are especially interested in the tail region. Fat right-tails have been extensively studied in insurance and finance [Wang, 1998; Embrechts *et al.*, 2009a,b; Degen *et al.*, 2010; Nam *et al.*, 2011; Chen *et al.*, 2012] and the behavior of aggregate risks in the tail region has received huge attention by researchers in last years [Cheung, 2009; Song and Yan, 2009; Hua and Joe, 2012]. To the best of our knowledge, however, previous studies of the subadditivity of risk measures in the tail region are scarce [Danielsson *et al.*, 2005; Hua and Joe, 2012].

3.6   Concavity of the distortion function

The subadditivity characteristic in the whole domain is in general not satisfied by GlueVaR risk measures. It was showed that GlueVaR risk measures can be interpreted as a linear combination of a highly conservative scenario, a conservative scenario and a less conservative scenario. We argued that a particular risk attitude is reflected depending on how these scenarios are weighted.

Given α and β, the other two parameters are directly related to the weights given to these scenarios. The shaded areas in Figure 3.2 delimit feasible weights (ω_1, ω_2) for GlueVaR$_{\beta,\alpha}^{\omega_1,\omega_2}$. For instance, it could be said that the three components of GlueVaR in expression (3.4) are equally important, that is, $\omega_1 = \omega_2 = \omega_3 = 1/3$. The point $(1/3, 1/3)$ in Figure 3.2 corresponds to the balanced risk attitude on the part of risk managers when faced by the three components shown in (3.4). The corresponding distortion function $\kappa_{\beta,\alpha}^{\omega_1,\omega_2}$ is concave on $[0, 1 - \alpha)$ in the lightly shaded area. Yet, the distortion function is not concave on $[0, 1 - \alpha)$ in the darkly shaded area. The distortion function is concave in $[0, 1]$ in the boldest continuous segment and, thus, the associated GlueVaR risk measure is subadditive.

Note that any pair of weights (ω_1, ω_2) on the boldest line in Figure 3.2 leads to $\omega_3 = 0$. This means that a zero weight is allocated to the least conservative scenario, i.e. the one associated with the VaR$_\alpha(X)$. This is indicative of the decision makers' conservative approach. Nonetheless, differences in just how restrictive this conservative attitude is can be found among the weights lying on this line: the nearer to $(\omega_1, \omega_2) = \left(\dfrac{\beta - 1}{\beta - \alpha}, \dfrac{1 - \alpha}{\beta - \alpha} \right)$, the less restrictive it is, while the nearer to $(\omega_1, \omega_2) = (1, 0)$, the more conservative it is.

If $\omega_1 < 0$, risk managers are optimistic regarding the impossibility of the occurrence of the worst case scenario, and so attach a negative weight to it.

3.7   Example of risk measurement with GlueVaR

Data for the cost of claims involving three type of damages described in the previous chapter are used to illustrate the application of GlueVaR risk measures in risk measurement. The sample consists of $n = 350$ observations of the cost of individual claims in thousands of euros. In Table 3.3 a set of quantile-based risk measures including three different GlueVaR are displayed. The table displays the corresponding risk figures for the cost of claims for property damage (X_1), the cost of claims of bodily injuries (X_2), the cost of claims of medical expenses (X_3) and the aggregate cost of claims $(X_1 + X_2 + X_3)$.

The selection of the three GlueVaR risk measures included in Table 3.3 de-

Figure 3.2   **Given α and β, the shaded areas delimits feasible weights (ω_1, ω_2) for GlueVaR$_{\beta,\alpha}^{\omega_1,\omega_2}$.**

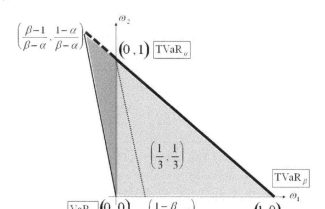

serves further explanation. The two confidence levels considered are $\alpha = 95\%$ and $\beta = 99.5\%$. The heights (h_1, h_2) are $(11/30, 2/3)$, $(0, 1)$ and $(1/20, 1/8)$ respectively. Different attitudes in front of the three scenarios of risk assessment are represented. GlueVaR$_{99.5\%,95\%}^{11/30,2/3}$ corresponds to a balanced attitude because the three quantile-based risk measures TVaR$_{99.5\%}$, TVaR$_{95\%}$ and VaR$_{95\%}$ are equally important, i.e. $\omega_1 = \omega_2 = \omega_3 = 1/3$. A different attitude is symbolized by GlueVaR$_{99.5\%,95\%}^{0,1}$ with associated weights $\omega_1 = -1/9$, $\omega_2 = 10/9$ and $\omega_3 = 0$. It corresponds to a scenario in which the manager overweights TVaR$_{95\%}$ and allocates the lowest feasible weight to TVaR$_{99.5\%}$ given that a zero weight is allocated to VaR$_{95\%}$. Finally, GlueVaR$_{99.5\%,95\%}^{1/20,1/8}$ reflects a risk measurement attitude just a bit more conservative than the one represented by using VaR$_{95\%}$, assigning low weights to TVaR$_{99.5\%}$ and TVaR$_{95\%}$ ($\omega_1 = 1/24$ and $\omega_2 = 1/12$).

As it is shown in Table 3.3, GlueVaR$_{99.5\%,95\%}^{11/30,2/3}$ is more conservative than the other two selected GlueVaR risk measures. This result can be generalized to all situations because the associated distortion function of GlueVaR$_{99.5\%,95\%}^{11/30,2/3}$ is greater than the other two distortion functions in the whole domain. Note that it is also observed in Table 3.3 that

$$\text{GlueVaR}_{99.5\%,95\%}^{1/20,1/8} \leq \text{GlueVaR}_{99.5\%,95\%}^{0,1}.$$

It is only valid to these data and an ordering between them can not be generalized. However, a relationship between these two GlueVaR risk measures

Table 3.3   Quantile-based risk measures and subadditivity

	X_1	X_2	X_3	$X_1 + X_2 + X_3$	Difference[(*)]
	(a)	(b)	(c)	(d)	(a+b+c-d)
$\mathrm{VaR}_{95\%}$	2.5	0.6	1.1	5.9	-1.7
$\mathrm{TVaR}_{95\%}$	12.5	8.0	1.3	19.7	2.1
$\mathrm{TVaR}_{99.5\%}$	40.8	42.1	1.8	81.1	3.6
$\mathrm{GlueVaR}_{99.5\%,95\%}^{11/30,2/3}$	18.6	16.9	1.4	35.6	1.9
$\mathrm{GlueVaR}_{99.5\%,95\%}^{1/20,1/8}$	4.9	2.9	1.1	10.2	-1.3
$\mathrm{GlueVaR}_{99.5\%,95\%}^{0,1}$	9.4	4.2	1.2	12.9	1.9

[(*)] Benefit of diversification.

and quantile-based risk measures can be established. It has been shown that

$$\mathrm{VaR}_\alpha \leqslant \mathrm{GlueVaR}_{\beta,\alpha}^{h_1,h_2} \leqslant \mathrm{TVaR}_\alpha \ \text{ if } \ h_1 \leqslant \frac{1-\beta}{1-\alpha}.$$

That means,

$$\mathrm{VaR}_{95\%} \leqslant \mathrm{GlueVaR}_{99.5\%,95\%}^{0,1} \leqslant \mathrm{TVaR}_{95\%}, \text{ because } 0 \leqslant 0.1, \text{ and}$$
$$\mathrm{VaR}_{95\%} \leqslant \mathrm{GlueVaR}_{99.5\%,95\%}^{1/20,1/8} \leqslant \mathrm{TVaR}_{95\%}, \text{ because } 0.05 \leqslant 0.1.$$

Although results in Table 3.3 may suggest that

$$\mathrm{TVaR}_{95\%} \leqslant \mathrm{GlueVaR}_{99.5\%,95\%}^{11/30,2/3} \leqslant \mathrm{TVaR}_{99.5\%},$$

this can not be asserted in general because conditions on the parameters of the GlueVaR risk measure to satisfy

$$\mathrm{TVaR}_\alpha \leqslant \mathrm{GlueVaR}_{\beta,\alpha}^{h_1,h_2} \leqslant \mathrm{TVaR}_\beta$$

$$\text{are } \frac{1-\beta}{1-\alpha} \leqslant h_1 \text{ and } h_2 = 1.$$

In this case it holds that $0.1 \leqslant 0.37$ but $h_2 \neq 1$.

Let us analyze the subadditivity property. Like the $VaR_{95\%}$, note that the $GlueVaR_{99.5\%,95\%}^{1/20,1/8}$ fails to be subadditive for X_1, X_2 and X_3 since $4.9+2.9+1.1 < 10.2$. Let us emphasize that these three GlueVaR risk measures have not associated a concave distortion function in the whole domain, so the subadditivity property can not be guaranteed for any of them. The fact that risk values are subadditive for the $GlueVaR_{99.5\%,95\%}^{11/30,2/3}$ and $GlueVaR_{99.5\%,95\%}^{0,1}$ is a characteristic attributable to this data but cannot be generalized to all contexts. In the case of the $GlueVaR_{99.5\%,95\%}^{11/30,2/3}$ and $GlueVaR_{99.5\%,95\%}^{1/20,1/8}$, the associated distortion function is concave in $[0, 1-\alpha)$.

3.8   Exercises

1. Consider the following empirical distribution

$$13,\ 15,\ 26,\ 26,\ 26,\ 37,\ 37,\ 100$$

   Determine the $GlueVaR_{85\%,50\%}^{11/30,2/3}$ and $GlueVaR_{85\%,50\%}^{0,1}$.

   Hint: The heights (h_1, h_2) equal to $(11/30, 2/3)$ and $(0, 1)$ correspond to $(\omega_1 = 1/3, \omega_2 = 1/3)$ and $(\omega_1 = -1/9, \omega_2 = 10/9)$, respectively.

2. Consider the following distribution function $F(x) = \frac{x^2}{9}$ for $0 < x \leqslant 3$. Find the $GlueVaR_{99.5\%,95\%}^{1/20,1/8}$.

   Hint: The heights (h_1, h_2) equal to $(1/20, 1/8)$ correspond to $\omega_1 = 1/24$ and $\omega_2 = 1/12$.

3. (Exemple 6.7 in [McNeil *et al.*, 2005]) Consider a defaultable corporate bond. The default probability is equal to 2%. The current price of the bond is 100. If there is no default, a bond pays in $t+1$ an amount of 105, otherwise there is no payment. Hence L the loss of bond is equal to 100 when the bond defaults and to -5 otherwise. Compute the $VaR_{95\%}$ of the following two portfolios:

   · Portfolio A consists of 100 units of this bond.
   · Portfolio B consists of 100 independent bonds with the same characteristics that this bond.

   Hint: The loss function of a bond can be expressed as $L = 100Y - 5(1 - Y) = 105Y - 5$, where Y is a indicator variable that takes value 1 if the bond defaults and 0 otherwise.

4. Let X and Y be two independent random variables uniformly distributed between $[0, 1]$ and $Z = X + Y$ their sum. Analyze if it holds that $\text{VaR}_{25\%}(Z) < \text{VaR}_{25\%}(X_1) + \text{VaR}_{25\%}(X_2)$.

   Hint: The cumulative distribution function of Z is

$$F_Z(z) = \begin{cases} \dfrac{z^2}{2} & \text{if } 0 < z \leqslant 1 \\[2mm] -\dfrac{z^2}{2} + 2z - 1 & \text{if } 1 < z \leqslant 2 \end{cases}$$

4   GlueVaR and other new risk measures

This chapter is structured in two parts. Analytical closed-form expressions of GlueVaR risk measures for commonly used statistical distributions in the insurance context are derived. These closed-form expressions should enable practitioners to undertake an effortless transition from the use of VaR and TVaR to GlueVaR. Third order Cornish-Fisher approximations to Glue-VaR risk measures for general skewed distribution functions are also introduced in this chapter. Finally, the relationship between GlueVaR, Tail Distortion risk measures and RVaR risk measures are shown.

4.1   Analytical closed-form expressions of GlueVaR

A useful consequence of (3.4) is that when analytical closed-form expressions of $\text{VaR}_\alpha(X)$ and $\text{TVaR}_\alpha(X)$ are known for a random variable X, the closed-form expression of $\text{GlueVaR}_{\beta,\alpha}^{h_1,h_2}(X)$ can automatically be derived without further complications. Otherwise, using the definition of GlueVaR as a distortion risk measure, the Choquet Integral of X with respect to the set function $\kappa_{\beta,\alpha}^{h_1,h_2} \circ P$ should be calculated.

4.1.1   Illustration: GlueVaR expression for Student t distribution

Let X be a random variable such that $\widetilde{X} = \dfrac{X - \mu}{\sigma}$ is distributed as a Student t random variable with v degrees of freedom (df). In such a case, X has μ mean and a standard deviation equal to $\sqrt{\dfrac{v \cdot \sigma^2}{v - 2}}$. Then

$$\text{VaR}_\alpha(X) = \mu + \sigma \cdot t_\alpha$$

$$\text{TVaR}_\alpha(X) = \mu + \sigma \cdot \frac{\tau(t_\alpha)}{1 - \alpha} \cdot \left(\frac{v + t_\alpha^2}{v - 1} \right),$$

where t_α is the α-quantile of a Student t distribution with ν df and τ is its density function.

Using (3.4) the GlueVaR of random variable X is

$$
\begin{aligned}
\text{GlueVaR}_{\beta,\alpha}^{h_1,h_2}(X) &= \omega_1 \cdot \left[\mu + \sigma \cdot \frac{\tau(t_\beta)}{1-\beta} \cdot \left(\frac{\nu + t_\beta^2}{\nu - 1} \right) \right] \\
&+ \omega_2 \cdot \left[\mu + \sigma \cdot \frac{\tau(t_\alpha)}{1-\alpha} \cdot \left(\frac{\nu + t_\alpha^2}{\nu - 1} \right) \right] + (1 - \omega_1 - \omega_2) \cdot (\mu + \sigma \cdot t_\alpha) \\
&= \mu + \sigma \cdot \left[\left(\frac{h_1}{1-\beta} - \frac{h_2 - h_1}{\beta - \alpha} \right) \cdot \tau(t_\beta) \cdot \left(\frac{\nu + t_\beta^2}{\nu - 1} \right) \right. \\
&\left. + \frac{h_2 - h_1}{\beta - \alpha} \cdot \tau(t_\alpha) \cdot \left(\frac{\nu + t_\alpha^2}{\nu - 1} \right) + (1 - h_2) \cdot t_\alpha \right].
\end{aligned}
$$

4.1.2 Analytical expressions for other frequently used distributions

Normal ($\mathcal{N}$), Lognormal ($\mathcal{LN}$) and Generalized Pareto ($\mathcal{GP}$) distributions have simple closed-form expressions of GlueVaR. The same notation conventions that were introduced in Chapter 1 are used. Namely, ϕ and Φ stand for the standard Normal pdf and cdf, respectively. The standard Normal distribution α and β quantiles are denoted as $q_\alpha = \Phi^{-1}(\alpha)$ and $q_\beta = \Phi^{-1}(\beta)$. For the $\mathcal{GP}$ distribution, the definition provided in Hosking and Wallis [1987] is considered, where the scale parameter is denoted by σ and k is the shape parameter. The $\mathcal{GP}$ distribution contains the Uniform ($k = 1$), the Exponential ($k = 0$), the Pareto ($k < 0$) and the type II Pareto ($k > 0$) distributions as special cases. Closed-form expressions of GlueVaR for several distributions are presented in Table 4.1. Note that there are some exceptions to the general rule to deduce these closed-form expressions to be considered. When X follows a Pareto distribution with $k \leqslant 1$ and for any confidence level α, $\text{TVaR}_\alpha(X) = +\infty$ as we have shown in Table 1.3 of Chapter 1. But when $h_1 = 0$ $\text{GlueVaR}_{\beta,\alpha}^{h_1,h_2}(X)$ is finite. There is a compensation effect between $\text{TVaR}_\alpha(X)$ and $\text{TVaR}_\beta(X)$. This is taken into account in Table 4.1.

Table 4.1   Closed-form expressions of GlueVaR for some selected distributions

Distribution	GlueVaR$_{\beta,\alpha}{}^{h_1,h_2}$ expression
Normal: $\mathcal{N}(\mu,\sigma^2)$	$\mu+\sigma\cdot q_\alpha\cdot(1-h_2)+\sigma\cdot\dfrac{h_2-h_1}{\beta-\alpha}\cdot[\phi(q_\alpha)-\phi(q_\beta)]+\sigma\cdot\dfrac{h_1}{1-\beta}\cdot$ $\phi(q_\beta)$
Lognormal: $\mathcal{LN}(\mu,\sigma^2)$	$\exp(\mu+\sigma\cdot q_\alpha)\cdot(1-h_2)$ $+\exp\left(\mu+\dfrac{\sigma^2}{2}\right)\cdot\dfrac{h_2-h_1}{\beta-\alpha}\cdot[\Phi(\sigma-q_\alpha)-\Phi(\sigma-q_\beta)]$ $+\exp\left(\mu+\dfrac{\sigma^2}{2}\right)\cdot\dfrac{h_1}{1-\beta}\cdot\Phi(\sigma-q_\beta)$
Exponential: $\mathcal{GP}(k,\sigma)$, with $k=0$	$\sigma\cdot[h_2-\ln(1-\alpha)]+\sigma\cdot(1-\beta)\cdot\ln\left(\dfrac{1-\beta}{1-\alpha}\right)\cdot\left[\dfrac{h_2-h_1}{\beta-\alpha}-\dfrac{h_1}{1-\beta}\right]$

Continued on next page

Table 4.1: continued from previous page

Distribution	GlueVaR$_{\beta,\alpha}{}^{h_1,h_2}$ expression
	$+\infty$ if $k \leqslant -1,\ h_1 \neq 0$
	$\dfrac{\sigma}{k} \cdot \left[1 - (1-\alpha)^k\right]$ $+\dfrac{h_2 - h_1}{\beta - \alpha} \cdot (1-\beta) \cdot \dfrac{\sigma}{k} \cdot \left[(1-\beta)^k - (1-\alpha)^k\right]$ $+\dfrac{h_2 - h_1}{\beta - \alpha} \cdot \dfrac{\sigma}{k+1} \cdot \left[(1-\alpha)^{k+1} - (1-\beta)^{k+1}\right]$ if $k < -1,\ h_1 = 0$
Pareto: $\mathcal{GP}(k,\sigma)$, with $k < 0$	$\sigma \cdot \left[\dfrac{1}{1-\alpha} - 1\right]$ $-\dfrac{h_2 - h_1}{\beta - \alpha} \cdot (1-\beta) \cdot \sigma \cdot \left[\dfrac{1}{1-\beta} - \dfrac{1}{1-\alpha}\right]$ $+\dfrac{h_2 - h_1}{\beta - \alpha} \cdot \sigma \cdot \ln\left(\dfrac{1-\alpha}{1-\beta}\right)$ if $k = -1,\ h_1 = 0$
	$\dfrac{\sigma}{k} \cdot [1 - (1-\alpha)^k]$ $+\dfrac{\sigma}{k} \cdot \left(\dfrac{h_2 - h_1}{\beta - \alpha} - \dfrac{h_1}{1-\beta}\right) \cdot [(1-\alpha)^k \cdot (1-\beta)]$ $+\dfrac{h_2 - h_1}{\beta - \alpha} \cdot \dfrac{\sigma}{k} \cdot \left[\dfrac{k \cdot (1-\alpha)^{k+1}}{k+1}\right]$ $+\left(\dfrac{h_2 - h_1}{\beta - \alpha} - \dfrac{h_1}{1-\beta}\right) \cdot \dfrac{\sigma}{k} \cdot \left[\dfrac{(1-\beta)^{k+1}}{k+1}\right]$ if $k \in (-1,0)$
Type II Pareto: $\mathcal{GP}(k,\sigma)$, with $k > 0$	$\dfrac{\sigma}{k} \cdot [1 - (1-\alpha)^k] + \dfrac{\sigma}{k} \cdot \left(\dfrac{h_2 - h_1}{\beta - \alpha} - \dfrac{h_1}{1-\beta}\right) \cdot [(1-\alpha)^k \cdot (1-\beta)]$ $+\dfrac{h_2 - h_1}{\beta - \alpha} \dfrac{\sigma}{k} \cdot \left[\dfrac{k \cdot (1-\alpha)^{k+1}}{k+1}\right]$ $+\left(\dfrac{h_2 - h_1}{\beta - \alpha} - \dfrac{h_1}{1-\beta}\right) \cdot \dfrac{\sigma}{k} \cdot \left[\dfrac{(1-\beta)^{k+1}}{k+1}\right]$

4.1.3   The Cornish-Fisher approximation of GlueVaR

General considerations about *Cornish-Fisher VaR* methodologies have been pointed out in Section 1.2.2 of Chapter 1. Approximations to GlueVaR risk measures for general skewed distribution functions using a Cornish-Fisher expansion of their quantiles are provided in this section. In insurance applications managers often have to face to highly skewed random variables with right fat tails. In many of these situations, however, they do not know whether the underlying random variable of interest is distributed according to a known parametric distribution function. In those situations that the distribution is unknown, the value of the common quantile-based risk measures is routinely approximated by practitioners. It is shown that approximations of GlueVaR risk measures for general unknown skewed distribution functions can be directly obtained by means of the relationship of GlueVaR risk measures and the standard quantile-based risk measures.

The Cornish-Fisher expansion is widely used by practitioners to approximate the $\mathrm{VaR}_\alpha(X)$ and $\mathrm{TVaR}_\alpha(X)$ values when the random variable follows a skewed unknown distribution [see Cornish and Fisher, 1937; Fisher and Cornish, 1960; Johnson and Kotz, 1970; McCune and Gray, 1982]. The VaR and TVaR measure values can be approximated as $\mathrm{VaR}_\alpha(X) \simeq \mu + q_{v,\alpha}\sigma$ and $\mathrm{TVaR}_\alpha(X) \simeq \mu + q_{tv,\alpha}\sigma$, where $\mu = \mathbb{E}[X]$, $\sigma^2 = \mathbb{V}[X]$ and both $q_{v,\alpha}$ and $q_{tv,\alpha}$ are modified quantiles of the standard Normal distribution that take into account the skewness of the distribution function of X.

Following Sandström [2007], the modified quantiles $q_{v,\alpha}$ and $q_{tv,\alpha}$ are computed as follows. Let us consider $\gamma = \mathbb{E}[(X-\mu)^3]/\sigma^3$ as a measure of the skewness of the random variable X. If $q_\alpha = \Phi^{-1}(\alpha)$ and ϕ are the α-quantile and the density function of the standard Normal distribution, respectively, then $q_{v,\alpha}$ and $q_{tv,\alpha}$ can be written as,

$$q_{v,\alpha} = \Phi^{-1}(\alpha) + \frac{\gamma}{6}\left[\left(\Phi^{-1}(\alpha)\right)^2 - 1\right] = q_\alpha + \frac{\gamma}{6}\left[q_\alpha^2 - 1\right],$$

$$q_{tv,\alpha} = \frac{\phi\left(\Phi^{-1}(\alpha)\right)}{1-\alpha}\left[1 + \frac{\gamma}{6}\left(\Phi^{-1}(\alpha)\right)^3\right] = \frac{\phi(q_\alpha)}{1-\alpha}\left[1 + \frac{\gamma}{6}q_\alpha^3\right].$$

Extensions of the Cornish-Fisher expansion that consider moments of higher order than γ have been provided in the literature [see, for instance, Giamouridis, 2006]. More details can be found in Appendix B of Sandström [2011].

Given the interpretation of a GlueVaR risk measure as a linear combination of risk measures which was shown in (3.4), the approximation for the GlueVaR of the random variable X following the Cornish-Fisher expansion can be obtained as

$$\text{GlueVaR}_{\beta,\alpha}^{h_1,h_2}(X) \simeq \mu + \sigma\left[\left(\frac{h_1}{1-\beta} - \frac{h_2-h_1}{\beta-\alpha}\right)\phi(q_\beta)\left(1+\frac{\gamma}{6}q_\beta^3\right)\right.$$
$$\left.+ \left(\frac{h_2-h_1}{\beta-\alpha}\right)\phi(q_\alpha)\left(1+\frac{\gamma}{6}q_\alpha^3\right) + (1-h_2)\left(\frac{\gamma}{6}\left(q_\alpha^2-1\right)+q_\alpha\right)\right].$$

The error of the approximation is upper bounded by the maximum error incurred when approximating $\text{VaR}_\alpha(X)$, $\text{TVaR}_\alpha(X)$ and $\text{TVaR}_\beta(X)$ using the equivalent Cornish-Fisher expansion for skewed distributions. This result is straightforward. It follows from the linear relationship shown in expression (3.4) and taking into account that weights ω_1, ω_2 and ω_3 are lower or equal than one, satisfying that $\omega_1 + \omega_2 + \omega_3 = 1$.

4.2 On the relationship between GlueVaR and Tail Distortion risk measures

As it has been aforementioned, different works that pay attention to risk measures based on distortion functions or based on several generalizations of quantiles have appeared in recent years. See, for instance, Zhu and Li [2012]; Bellini and Gianin [2012]; Bellini *et al.* [2014]; Dhaene *et al.* [2012a] and Goovaerts *et al.* [2012].

This section is devoted to reveal the connections between GlueVaR risk measures and Tail Distortion risk measures. To the best of our knowledge, Tail Distortion risk measures were introduced in Zhu and Li [2012]. Here the notation used for these family of risk measures is adapted from that in Lv *et al.* [2013]. Consider a distortion function g, this is a non-decreasing and injective function g from $[0,1]$ to $[0,1]$ such that $g(0) = 0$ and $g(1) = 1$, and a confidence level $\alpha \in (0,1)$. The Tail Distortion Risk Measure $T_{g,\alpha}$ associated to g and α is defined as the distortion risk measure with distortion function g_α, where

$$g_\alpha(u) = g\left(\frac{u}{1-\alpha}\right) \cdot \mathbb{1}[0 \leqslant u < 1-\alpha] + \mathbb{1}[1-\alpha \leqslant u \leqslant 1].$$

Note that $\mathbb{1}[0 \leqslant u < 1-\alpha]$ is a function that takes value 1 in the interval $[0 \leqslant u < 1-\alpha]$ and 0 elsewhere. In other words, if X is a random variable representing a loss in a probability space $(\Omega, \mathscr{A}, P)$ and its survival function is $S_X(x) = P(X > x)$, then

$$T_{g,\alpha}(X) = \int_{-\infty}^{0} [g_\alpha(S_X(x)) - 1] \, dx + \int_{0}^{+\infty} g_\alpha(S_X(x)) \, dx. \qquad (4.1)$$

Note that g_α is continuous in $1 - \alpha$ or, alternatively, $g_\alpha(1 - \alpha) = 1$.

Proposition 4.1. *Consider a* GlueVaR$_{\beta,\alpha}^{\omega_1,\omega_2}$ *risk measure with parameters* α, β, ω_1 *and* ω_2. *This GlueVaR is equivalent to a Tail Distortion risk measure* $T_{g,\alpha}$ *if, and only if,* $\omega_2 = 1 - \omega_1$ *and*

$$
g(t) = \left(\frac{\omega_1 \cdot (1 - \alpha)}{1 - \beta} + 1 - \omega_1 \right) \cdot t \cdot \mathbb{1}\left[0 \leqslant t < (1 - \alpha)^{-1} \cdot (1 - \beta) \right]
$$
$$
+ (\omega_1 + (1 - \omega_1) \cdot t) \cdot \mathbb{1}\left[(1 - \alpha)^{-1} \cdot (1 - \beta) \leqslant t \leqslant 1 \right]. \qquad (4.2)
$$

The proof is provided in Section A.3 of the Appendix.

Note that only GlueVaR risk measures with $\omega_3 = 0$ can be represented as Tail Distortion risk measures, because $\omega_1 + \omega_2 + \omega_3 = 1$ must hold as part of the definition of a GlueVaR$_{\beta,\alpha}^{\omega_1,\omega_2}$ risk measure. In other words, one can only represent as Tail Distortion risk measures those GlueVaR that do not weight the part corresponding to the VaR$_\alpha$.

The origin of GlueVaR risk measures can be found in Belles-Sampera [2011]. As a curiosity, the definition of a parametric family of risk measures named PUp-TVaR can also be found therein, which are exactly the Tail Distortion risk measures linked to Proportional Hazards Distortion functions $g(u) = u^{\frac{1}{a}}$, $a \geqslant 1$ from the perspective of Zhu and Li [2012].

4.3   On the relationship between GlueVaR and RVaR risk measures

To the best of our knowledge RVaR risk measures were introduced in Cont *et al.* [2010]. This section is dedicated to show a close relationship between GlueVaR risk measures and the RVaR family. We have recently discovered this connection. It is highly probable that some synergies between the research associated to both families are going to arise. For instance, existing results related to capital allocation principles using RVaR [see, for instance, Embrechts *et al.*, 2016] and the ones obtained with GlueVaR (which we are going to present in Chapter 7) may be interconnected. Another example of these synergies may be found in the analysis of risk attitudes that we present in Chapter 5 because, as we will show, the application of our assessment tools are straightforward in RVaR risk measures.

Let X be an absolutely continuous random variable, which positive values represent losses. Let α, $\beta \in [0, 1]$. The value of the risk measure RVaR$_{\alpha,\beta}$

applied to X is, by definition, the following:

$$\text{RVaR}_{\alpha,\beta}(X) = \begin{cases} \dfrac{1}{\beta} \displaystyle\int_{\alpha}^{\alpha+\beta} \text{VaR}_{\gamma}(X)\,d\gamma & \text{if } \beta > 0 \\ \text{VaR}_{\alpha}(X) & \text{if } \beta = 0 \end{cases} \tag{4.3}$$

The notation used for VaR is not the one used when defining GlucVaR risk measures, because $\text{VaR}_{\alpha}(X)$ in (4.3) refers to the $100(1-\alpha)\%$ quantile while in GlueVaR definition the notation $\text{VaR}_{\alpha}(X)$ is used to representing the $100\alpha\%$ quantile. In order to find relationships between RVaR and GlueVaR risk measures it is convenient to rewrite expression (4.3) as

$$\text{RVaR}_{\alpha,\beta}(X) = \begin{cases} \dfrac{1}{\beta} \displaystyle\int_{\alpha}^{\alpha+\beta} \text{VaR}_{1-\gamma}(X)\,d\gamma & \text{if } \beta > 0 \\ \text{VaR}_{1-\alpha}(X) & \text{if } \beta = 0 \end{cases} \tag{4.4}$$

The notation used in definition of GlueVaR risk measures for VaR is incorporated in (4.4).

Note that

$$\begin{aligned} \frac{1}{\beta} \int_{\alpha}^{\alpha+\beta} \text{VaR}_{1-\gamma}(X)\,d\gamma &= \frac{1}{\beta} \int_{1-(\alpha+\beta)}^{1-\alpha} \text{VaR}_{\lambda}(X)\,d\lambda \\ &= \frac{1}{\beta} \left[\int_{1-(\alpha+\beta)}^{1} \text{VaR}_{\lambda}(X)\,d\lambda - \int_{1-\alpha}^{1} \text{VaR}_{\lambda}(X)\,d\lambda \right] \\ \overset{\substack{\text{notation used in def. of} \\ \text{GlueVaR}}}{=} \frac{1}{\beta} &\left[(\alpha+\beta)\text{TVaR}_{1-(\alpha+\beta)}(X) - \alpha\text{TVaR}_{1-\alpha}(X) \right] \\ &= \frac{\alpha+\beta}{\beta} \text{TVaR}_{1-(\alpha+\beta)}(X) - \frac{\alpha}{\beta}\text{TVaR}_{1-\alpha}(X) \quad (4.5) \end{aligned}$$

Let us introduce some additional notation: $a = 1 - \alpha$ and $b = 1 - \beta$. So it can be deduced that $1 - (\alpha + \beta) = a + b - 1$ and that $\alpha + \beta = 2 - (a + b)$. Therefore, last expression in (4.5) may be rewritten as

$$\frac{2-(a+b)}{1-b}\text{TVaR}_{a+b-1}(X) - \frac{1-a}{1-b}\text{TVaR}_{a}(X) \tag{4.6}$$

Note now that $a + b - 1 \leq a$ because $a, b \in [0,1]$, and this implies that $\text{TVaR}_{a}(X) \geq \text{TVaR}_{a+b-1}(X)$. Additionally, if

$$\omega_1 = -\frac{1-a}{1-b} \text{ and } \omega_2 = \frac{2-(a+b)}{1-b} \tag{4.7}$$

then $\omega_1 + \omega_2 = \dfrac{1}{1-b}[a-1+2-a-b] = \dfrac{1-b}{1-b} = 1.$

Recall that a usual way to write the value of a GlueVaR risk measure applied to X is as follows:

$$\text{GlueVaR}_{\widehat{\beta},\widehat{\alpha}}^{\widehat{h_1},\widehat{h_2}}(X) = \widehat{\omega_1}\text{TVaR}_{\widehat{\beta}}(X) + \widehat{\omega_2}\text{TVaR}_{\widehat{\alpha}}(X)$$

$$+ (1 - \widehat{\omega_1} - \widehat{\omega_2})\text{VaR}_{\widehat{\alpha}}(X) \qquad (4.8)$$

where $\widehat{\omega_1}$ and $\widehat{\omega_2}$ depend on parameters $\widehat{\alpha}$, $\widehat{\beta}$, $\widehat{h_1}$ and $\widehat{h_2}$.
Taking into account the previous expressions and notations, consider

$$\begin{aligned}
\widehat{\alpha} &= a + b - 1 \\
\widehat{\beta} &= a \\
\widehat{\omega_1} = \omega_1 &= -\frac{1-a}{1-b} \\
\widehat{\omega_2} = \omega_2 &= \frac{2-(a+b)}{1-b}.
\end{aligned} \qquad (4.9)$$

As long as $\widehat{\omega_1}$ and $\widehat{\omega_2}$ are related to $\widehat{h_1}$ and $\widehat{h_2}$ by the next expression (as it is shown in Section A.2 of the Appendix)

$$\begin{pmatrix} \widehat{h_1} \\ \widehat{h_2} \end{pmatrix} = \begin{pmatrix} 1 & \frac{1-\widehat{\beta}}{1-\widehat{\alpha}} \\ 1 & 1 \end{pmatrix} \begin{pmatrix} \widehat{\omega_1} \\ \widehat{\omega_2} \end{pmatrix} \qquad (4.10)$$

it is deduced from (4.9) and (4.10) that

$$\begin{aligned}
\widehat{h_1} &= -\frac{1-a}{1-b} + \left[\frac{2-(a+b)}{1-b}\right]\frac{1-a}{2-(a+b)} = \frac{-(1-a)+(1-a)}{1-b} = 0 \\
\widehat{h_2} &= -\frac{1-a}{1-b} + \left[\frac{2-(a+b)}{1-b}\right] = \frac{1-b}{1-b} = 1
\end{aligned} \qquad (4.11)$$

So, putting (4.8), (4.9) and (4.11) altogether the following expression holds:

$$\text{GlueVaR}_{a,a+b-1}^{0,1}(X) = -\frac{1-a}{1-b}\text{TVaR}_a(X)$$

$$+ \frac{2-(a+b)}{1-b}\text{TVaR}_{a+b-1}(X). \qquad (4.12)$$

The right-hand side of expression (4.12) is exactly expression (4.6). This means that, for $\beta > 0$ (or, equivalently, for $b < 1$),

$$\text{RVaR}_{\alpha,\beta} = \text{GlueVaR}_{a,a+b-1}^{0,1}.$$

For $\beta = 0$ (or $b = 1$), expression (4.12) is not well defined, but $a+b-1 = a$ in such a case and it can be checked that $\text{GlueVaR}_{a,a}^{0,1} = \text{VaR}_a$. To get the feeling that this is correct, let us plot the distortion function of $\text{GlueVaR}_{a,a+b-1}^{0,1}$ in Figure 4.1.

Figure 4.1   Distortion function of GlueVaR$_{a,a+b-1}^{0,1}$ distortion risk measure.

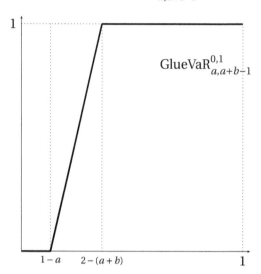

Looking at the plot of the distortion function in Figure 4.1, if $b = 1$ then $2 - (a + b) = 1 - a$ and then the distortion function of VaR$_a$ would appear. In addition, if $a = 1$ (which means that $\alpha = 0$) then the distortion function of TVaR$_b$ is obtained. As it is one of the purposes of RVaR$_{\alpha,\beta}$ risk measures, it is possible to continuously moving from VaR$_{1-\alpha}$ to TVaR$_{1-\beta}$.

Taking all the previous comments into account, the following equivalence holds:

$$RVaR_{\alpha,\beta} = GlueVaR_{a,a+b-1}^{0,1} \tag{4.13}$$

4.4   Example

The example of risk quantification shown in Chapter 3 is followed to estimate GlueVaR risk measures considering alternative distributions. Outcomes are shown in Table 4.2. The table is divided into four blocks, each block representing the corresponding risk figures for the cost of claims for property damage (X_1), the cost of claims of bodily injuries (X_2), the cost of claims of medical expenses (X_3) and the aggregate cost of claims ($X_1 + X_2 + X_3$). Risk measure values using the empirical distribution (first row) are compared with outcomes when Normal, Lognormal, Student t with 4 df and Generalized Pareto distributions are fitted to data. In the last two rows of each block results are shown when risk measure values are approximated by a Cornish-Fisher expansion. The sample mean ($\hat{\mu} = \bar{z}$), the sample deviation ($\hat{\sigma}^2 = \sum_i (Z_i - \bar{z})^2 / (n-1)$) and the sample skewness (calculated as $\hat{\gamma} = \hat{\sigma}^{-3} (\sum_i (Z_i - \bar{z})^3 / n)$) are considered as estimators of μ, σ and γ when Z is one of the four random variables X_1, X_2, X_3, $X_1 + X_2 + X_3$. Sample statistics were computed using observations that fall below the 99.5% quantile in order to exclude the effect of extreme losses on estimates (first Cornish-Fisher approximation). That means, a subsample of the first 348 increasingly ordered elements of the random variable were used to estimate parameters. Therefore, the two highest values were considered as extreme losses and were not included. Outcome values of risk measures were compared with the risk measure approximations when all the observations are included on sample estimates (second Cornish-Fisher approximation). All the calculations were made in R and MS Excel.

Table 4.2   Examples of risk measurement of costs of insurance claims using quantile-based risk measures

Model	VaR$_{95\%}$	TVaR$_{95\%}$	TVaR$_{99.5\%}$	GlueVaR$^{h_1,h_2}_{99.5\%,95\%}$ $\left(\frac{11}{30}, \frac{2}{3}\right)$	$(0,1)$	$\left(\frac{1}{20}, \frac{1}{8}\right)$
X_1						
Empirical	2.5	12.5	40.8	18.6	9.4	4.9
Normal	6.9	8.5	11.6	9.0	8.1	7.2
Lognormal	2.7	8.7	32.7	14.5	5.4	4.4
Student t (4 d.f.)	8.8	12.8	24.6	15.4	11.5	9.8
Pareto	2.5	5.5	18.1	8.7	4.1	3.4
Cornish-Fisher[1a]	8.5	27.8	128.4	54.9	16.6	15.1
Cornish-Fisher[1b]	16.3	59.1	284.0	119.8	34.1	31.0
X_2						
Empirical	0.6	8.0	42.1	16.9	4.2	2.9
Normal	6.0	7.4	10.2	7.9	7.1	6.3
Lognormal	1.6	5.8	25.7	11.0	3.6	3.0
Student t (4 d.f.)	7.6	11.2	21.7	13.5	10.1	8.5
Pareto	1.6	3.5	11.9	5.7	2.6	2.2
Cornish-Fisher[2a]	2.2	2.7	3.7	2.9	2.6	2.3
Cornish-Fisher[2b]	6.1	7.5	10.3	8.0	7.2	6.4
X_3						
Empirical	1.1	1.3	1.8	1.4	1.2	1.1

Continued on next page

Table 4.2: continued from previous page

Model	VaR$_{95\%}$	TVaR$_{95\%}$	TVaR$_{99.5\%}$	GlueVaR$_{99.5\%,95\%}^{h_1,h_2}$ $\left(\frac{11}{30},\frac{2}{3}\right)$	$(0,1)$	$\left(\frac{1}{20},\frac{1}{8}\right)$
Normal	0.9	1.0	1.3	1.1	1.0	0.9
Lognormal	0.8	1.4	3.2	1.8	1.2	1.0
Student t (4 d.f.)	1.0	1.4	2.5	1.7	1.3	1.1
Pareto	0.9	1.4	3.0	1.8	1.2	1.0
Cornish-Fisher$^{(3a)}$	1.0	2.1	7.6	3.6	1.5	1.4
Cornish-Fisher$^{(3b)}$	1.1	2.0	6.1	3.1	1.5	1.4
$X_1 + X_2 + X_3$						
Empirical	5.9	19.7	81.1	35.6	12.9	10.2
Normal	12.6	15.4	21.1	16.4	14.8	13.2
Lognormal	5.5	15.8	60.7	27.3	10.8	8.6
Student t (4 d.f.)	16.0	23.2	44.4	27.8	20.8	17.7
Pareto	5.0	11.0	36.0	17.3	8.1	6.7
Cornish-Fisher$^{(4a)}$	11.0	34.3	155.5	66.9	20.8	19.0
Cornish-Fisher$^{(4b)}$	34.6	134.0	659.7	276.1	75.6	68.9

$^{(1a)}$ $\widehat{\mu}=0.5$, $\widehat{\sigma}=2.3$ and $\widehat{\gamma}=6.4$. Subsample without extreme losses. The two largest values of X_1 are excluded.

$^{(1b)}$ $\widehat{\mu}=0.7$, $\widehat{\sigma}=3.8$ and $\widehat{\gamma}=8.7$. Full sample.

$^{(2a)}$ $\widehat{\mu}=0.2$, $\widehat{\sigma}=1.2$ and $\widehat{\gamma}=0$. Subsample without extreme losses. The two largest values of X_2 are excluded.

$^{(2b)}$ $\widehat{\mu}=0.5$, $\widehat{\sigma}=3.4$ and $\widehat{\gamma}=0$. Full sample.

$^{(3a)}$ $\widehat{\mu}=0.3$, $\widehat{\sigma}=0.3$ and $\widehat{\gamma}=2.6$. Subsample without extreme losses. The two largest values of X_2 are excluded.

$^{(3b)}$ $\widehat{\mu}=0.3$, $\widehat{\sigma}=0.4$ and $\widehat{\gamma}=1.4$. Full sample.

$^{(4a)}$ $\widehat{\mu}=1.0$, $\widehat{\sigma}=3$ and $\widehat{\gamma}=5.9$. Subsample without extreme losses. The two largest values of $X_1 + X_2 + X_3$ are excluded.

$^{(4b)}$ $\widehat{\mu}=1.4$, $\widehat{\sigma}=6.8$ and $\widehat{\gamma}=11.4$. Full sample.

Some comments related to outcome values for Cornish-Fisher approximations of the quantile-based risk measures should be made. According to the results, one could think that this kind of risk measurement corresponds to a conservative attitude for the two types of approximations shown in Table 4.2. The exception would be risk values obtained when X_2 is evaluated.

Relevant differences are observed depending on the approximation finally used on right skewed data. Outcome values related to the second Cornish-Fisher approximation (full sample) are drastically large when the data are severely right skewed distributed, as in the case of X_1 and $X_1 + X_2 + X_3$. These outcome values would be associated to a excessively conservative (un-realistic) attitude. If the first Cornish-Fisher approximation is considered, i.e. when sample statistics were estimated excluding extreme losses, a sig-nificant drop is observed although the outcome values for this approxima-tion are still larger than those values associated with the empirical or the parametric distributions for right-skewed random variables. Note that only the two largest losses are not included in the sample estimates involving the first approximation. When the data are slightly right skewed distributed, as in the case of X_3, the two Cornish-Fisher approximations show a bet-ter performance. In other words, the Cornish-Fisher approximation should be used with certain caution when the data are severely right skewed dis-tributed. Probably higher order moments should be taken into account.

An important issue that arises from these results is the model risk. Even when the same risk measure is used, huge differences are observed depend-ing on the hypothesis about the underlying distribution of the claim cost random variables. Let us assume that the regulator is focused on the VaR$_{95\%}$ for the aggregate cost $X_1 + X_2 + X_3$ as a measure of pure underwriting risk (without taking into account the premium paid by the policyholders). If it is supposed that the random variable is Pareto distributed, then the institution will need 5 thousands of euros for regulatory solvency purposes. The com-pany should set aside almost 3.2 times this economic amount whether the underlying distribution is Student t with 4 degrees of freedom. This topic is out of the scope of this chapter. The interested reader is addressed, for instance, to the study of Alexander and Sarabia [2012] which deals with VaR model risk or to the reference Aggarwal *et al.* [2016] suggested at the end of Chapter 1.

4.5   Exercises

1. Determine if the GlueVaR$_{99.5\%,95\%}^{11/30,2/3}$ of a Normal distributed random vari-able X with $\mathcal{N}(\mu = 5, \sigma^2 = 16)$ satisfies the expressions related to the properties of *Translation invariance*, *Positive homogeneity* and *Strictness*.

2. Consider the Normal distributed random variable X_1 with $\mathcal{N}(\mu = 5, \sigma^2 = 16)$ and the Normal distributed random variable X_2 with $\mathcal{N}(\mu = 4, \sigma^2 = $

20). Show that:

- $\text{VaR}_\alpha(Z)$ is equal to $\text{VaR}_\alpha(X_1) + \text{VaR}_\alpha(X_2)$ for any α in the case that $r_{xy} = 1$, where $Z = X_1 + X_2$ and r_{xy} is the Pearson linear correlation coefficient.
- When $r_{xy} < 1$, then $\text{VaR}_\alpha(Z) < \text{VaR}_\alpha(X_1) + \text{VaR}_\alpha(X_2)$.
- Repeat the analysis for the $\text{GlueVaR}_{99.5\%,95\%}^{1/20,1/8}$ risk measure.

3. Check that if X is distributed as a Pareto ($X \sim \mathcal{GP}(k,\sigma)$, with $k < 0$), the expression for $\text{TVaR}_\alpha(X)$ shown in Table 1.3 may be obtained either:

- From Definition 1.9 (i.e, $\text{TVaR}_\alpha(X) = \dfrac{1}{1-\alpha} \displaystyle\int_\alpha^1 \text{VaR}_\lambda(X) d\lambda$), or
- From the expression of $\text{TVaR}_\alpha(X)$ as a distortion risk measure shown in Section 3.2 (i.e.

$$\text{TVaR}_\alpha(X) = \int_{-\infty}^0 \left[\gamma_\alpha(S_X(x)) - 1 \right] dx + \int_0^{+\infty} \gamma_\alpha(S_X(x)) \, dx,$$

where γ_α is the distortion function displayed in Table 3.2).

Hint: Note that, in this case,

$$\left(1 - \frac{k}{\sigma} \text{VaR}_\alpha(X) \right)^{1/k} = S_X(\text{VaR}_\alpha(X)) = 1 - \alpha.$$

4. Obtain the RVaR risk measure equivalent to the $\text{GlueVaR}_{95\%,90\%}^{0,1}$.

5   Risk measure choice

Tools designed to provide adequate risk measurements are needed by both decision making agents and regulatory agents, who require information about potential losses within a probabilistic framework. As such, the choice of a risk measure plays a central role in decision making in many areas including health, safety, environmental, adversarial and catastrophic risks [Cox Jr., L.A., 2013; MacKenzie, 2014]. Many different risk measures are available to practitioners, but the selection of the most suitable risk measure to be used in a given context is generally controversial. A key element in characterizing a risk measure is the underlying risk attitude that is assumed when this measure is used for risk assessment. Therefore, in selecting the best measure, the practitioner is concerned with how a particular measure matches up with the alternatives. However, this simple question only has a complex answer.

Consider the Value at Risk and the Tail Value at Risk, probably the most common risk measures used in assessing risk. Suppose α is the confidence level, which reflects the degree of tolerance to undesirable events. The $\mathrm{VaR}_\alpha(X)$ is the α-quantile of loss X, while the $\mathrm{TVaR}_\alpha(X)$ averages quantiles ranging from the α-quantile to the maximum (the 100%-quantile) of X. Based on these definitions, it seems obvious that these two quantile-based risk measures can be directly compared in terms of their respective conceptions of risk using their associated confidence levels. For instance, the VaR provides for a concept of risk associated with a barrier, beyond which the decision maker assumes that catastrophe lies [Alexander and Sarabia, 2012]. A VaR at a 95% confidence level presents a lower resistance to undesirable events than a VaR at a 99% level. This also holds for $\mathrm{TVaR}_\alpha(X)$. Comparisons of VaR and TVaR measures can likewise be readily undertaken when their respective confidence levels are fixed and equal. Given an α-confidence level, the $\mathrm{TVaR}_\alpha(X)$ is always greater or equal than the $\mathrm{VaR}_\alpha(X)$. However, a direct comparison cannot be made if the VaR and the TVaR risk measures have different confidence levels. For example, imagine a decision maker wishes to compare the implicit risk attitude of the $\text{TVaR}_{95\%}(X)$ and the $\text{VaR}_{99\%}(X)$. In this instance, it is not immediately obvious which of these two risk measures offers the greatest risk tolerance. Furthermore, if the decision maker wants to know the risk attitude of a measure other than that of these two quantile-based risk measures, comparisons are even less intuitive. Here, we focus on the family of distortion risk measures, where the VaR and TVaR can be understood as two particular cases. This chapter seeks to contribute to the study of attitudes towards risk in the assessment of risk. The study analyses the risk perception that is implicit when an agent applies a particular distortion risk measure. A battery of instruments is developed to facilitate the comparison of the risk attitude of distortion risk measures from both global and local perspectives. The results afford new elements for determining the suitability of a particular distortion risk measure in comparison with other available options. They also allow an agent to determine which risk measure provides the most risk tolerant behavior.

An illustrative example of the risk attitude characterization implicit in a distortion risk measure is included in this chapter. The European insurance regulatory framework serves as an excellent example of the choice of a compulsory risk measure, i.e. $\text{VaR}_{99.5\%}$. However, insurers implement other choices in their internal tools. We show that, given a particular insurer's dataset, distortion risk measures other than that of the Value at Risk can provide the same risk estimates. However, if the insurer does choose a different risk measure, this chapter provides complementary tools for evaluating risk that can be used to understand its position in the European insurance or financial market, or even to benchmark it in relation to the mandatory risk assessment standard.

5.1   Aggregate attitude towards risk

The characterization of the implicit attitude towards risk in a given distortion risk measure is carried out by means of the analysis of the distortion function, which provides a precise portrait of the underlying risk position of a decision maker when selecting a particular risk measure for risk assessment.

Let us consider the mathematical expectation. As indicated previously in Section 3.2 of Chapter 3, the mathematical expectation can be understood as a distortion risk measure involving the identity function id as the associated distortion function. Figure 5.1 illustrates the distortion function associated with the mathematical expectation. In other words, the mathematical expectation can be understood as the distortion risk measure used by agents when survival probabilities are not distorted (i.e. they are distorted by the identity function). So, the mathematical expectation can be associated with a risk neutral attitude of the agent.

Figure 5.1   Distortion function of the mathematical expectation

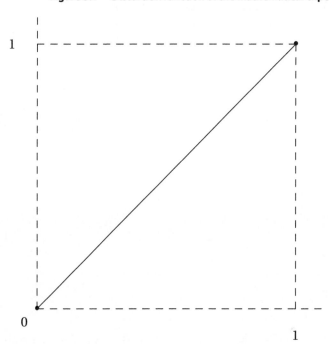

The area under the distortion function can be understood as an indicator of the *aggregate risk attitude* of an agent, with decision makers being classified as risk tolerant, risk neutral or risk intolerant. Note that we assume that a risk neutral agent would not distort the survival distribution function, so the associated distortion function linked to aggregated risk neutrality would be the id function. The area under the id function is one half and this value could be used as a benchmark of global risk attitude. A globally risk intolerant agent would make an upper distortion of the survival distribution in accumulated terms; thus, the area under g for this agent would be larger than one half. Similarly, an agent would be globally risk tolerant if the area under g was lower than one half.

The distortion functions of the Value at Risk and Tail Value at Risk with alpha confidence level are shown in Figure 5.2 and Figure 5.3, respectively. From

Figure 5.2 it is straightforward to check that the area under the distortion function of the VaR_α is α. Similarly, from Figure 5.3 it is easy to observe that the area under the distortion function of the TVaR_α is $\alpha + (1 - \alpha)/2$.

Figure 5.2   Distortion function of the VaR$_\alpha$ risk measure

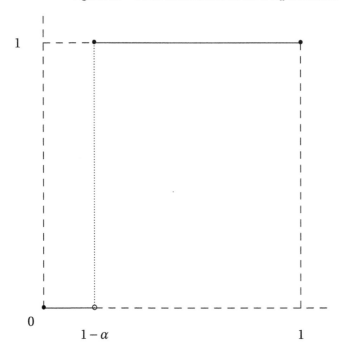

An agent would be globally risk neutral using either the VaR_α measure with $\alpha = 0.5$ or the TVaR_α with α equal to zero. In terms of aggregate risk neutrality it would be equivalent to use either the mathematical expectation, or $\text{VaR}_{50\%}$ or $\text{TVaR}_{0\%}$. Note that $\text{VaR}_{50\%}$ is the median and $\text{TVaR}_{0\%}$ is the mathematical expectation. Similarly, an agent would be globally risk intolerant using either the VaR_α with $\alpha > 0.5$ or the TVaR_α with a positive α. On the contrary, an agent would be globally risk tolerant using the VaR_α with $\alpha < 0.5$. It is worthy to emphasize that under the definition of aggregate risk attitude followed in this chapter an aggregate risk tolerant agent would never use the TVaR risk measure, since the area under the distortion function is bounded in the interval $[0.5, 1]$.

GlueVaR risk measures were introduced in Chapter 3 as a class of distortion risk measures. Recall that these measures are defined by means of four parameters α, β, ω_1 and ω_2, such that $0 < \alpha \leqslant \beta < 1$, $\dfrac{\beta - 1}{\beta - \alpha} \leqslant \omega_1 \leqslant 1$ and $\omega_1 +$

Figure 5.3   Distortion function of the TVaR$_\alpha$ risk measure

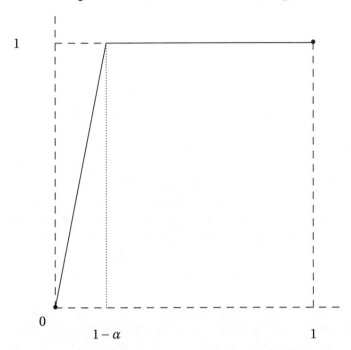

$\omega_2 \leqslant 1$. This parametric flexibility of GlueVaR risk measures makes them useful in a variety of contexts, because each particular risk context could require a different set of parameter values. In the case of the GlueVaR$_{\beta,\alpha}^{\omega_1,\omega_2}$, the implicit global risk attitude would depend on the values of the four parameters that define the risk measure.

To conclude, in Belles-Sampera *et al.* [2013b] we introduced some relationships between distortion risk measures and aggregation operators. Aggregation functions (or operators) are mathematical functions used for combining information in many fields of human knowledge, as artificial intelligence, biology or economics [Torra and Narukawa, 2007]. Aggregation indicators are used to characterize the aggregation function [Belles-Sampera *et al.*, 2014c, 2013c]. One of the most frequently used indicators is the degree of orness, which seeks to summarize the importance of each ith-order statistic, $i = 1, \ldots, n$, in the aggregation process associated with the Choquet integral with respect to a set function. This indicator provides some kind of *level of preference* inherent to such an aggregation function on a $[0, 1]$ scale, where 0 represents the minimum and 1 the maximum order statistic (Dujmović [2006]; Fernández Salido and Murakami [2003]). In Belles-Sampera *et al.* [2016c] we showed that the degree of orness can be interpreted as an approximation of the area under the distortion function.

5.1.1 Local risk attitude

It is reasonable to suppose that decision makers do not worry about all random event losses in the same way. Decision makers frequently treat different random events distinctly (note that some of these events can represent benefits or affordable losses). While the area under the distortion function evaluates the accumulated distortion performed over the survival distribution function, it does not take into account which part of the survival distribution function was distorted. Clearly, from the perspective of a manager, distorting the survival probability in the right tail of the random variable linked to losses is not the same as distorting the probability in the left tail. Additionally, all distortion functions with an area equal to one half would be associated with global risk neutrality, where the id function is only a particular case.

In Figure 5.4 it is shown an example in which the size of the area under several distortion functions is the same. Obviously, these distortion functions have not associated the same risk attitude. In the case of the distortion function represented by a dotted line, survival probability values in the interval $[0, 0.5]$ are overweighted and survival probability values in the interval $[0.5, 1]$ are underweighted. So, relatively high losses are overrepresented (right tail) and relatively low losses are underrepresented. On the contrary, the distortion function represented by the solid line overweights relatively low losses and underweights high losses. Note that also the area under the diagonal, which is in fact the distortion function of the mathematical expectation, is the same.

Therefore, the global vision of risk embedded in a risk measure has to be completed with local information. One option open to us is to define the risk attitude in absolute terms. An *absolute risk neutral agent* is a decision maker that does not distort the survival probability and who, therefore, uses the id function as the associated distortion function, i.e. $g(u) = \text{id}(u) = u$ for all $0 \leqslant u \leqslant 1$. An *absolute risk intolerant agent* is associated with a distortion function g such that $g(u) > u$, for all $0 \leqslant u \leqslant 1$. And, similarly, an *absolute risk tolerant agent* has a distortion function g such that $g(u) < u$, for all $0 \leqslant u \leqslant 1$. This definition of risk attitude is in absolute terms in the sense that the relationship of ordering between $g(u)$ and u must be fulfilled in the whole range $[0, 1]$. Note that these considerations lead to a more restrictive

Figure 5.4   Example of distortion functions with the same area

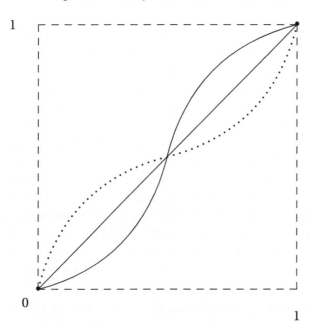

definition of risk attitude than that provided by the *aggregate risk attitude*. The definition of the absolute risk attitude implies that the implicit attitude of an agent is invariant over the range of values. Yet, there are no reasons as to why the agent should have a unique risk attitude across the whole domain. An agent's attitude to risk is likely to differ in accordance with the interval of loss under consideration. The risk attitude implicit in frequently used risk measures is not invariant; this is the case, for instance, of the VaR_α. When using the VaR_α, a risk intolerant attitude is associated with the interval $[1 - \alpha, 1)$, but a risk tolerant attitude is associated with the interval $(0, 1 - \alpha)$. Thus, an homogeneous risk attitude cannot be linked to the VaR_α risk measure throughout the domain.

Let us define a quotient function Q_g from $(0, 1]$ to $\mathbb{R}$, based on the distortion function g associated with the risk measure, in order to characterize the local vision of risk. Let the function Q_g be defined as the quotient between the distortion function g and the identity function, $Q_g(u) = \frac{g(u)}{u}$ for all $0 < u \le 1$. The Q_g allows the analysis of the agent's perception of risk at any point in the survival probability distribution. This quotient function provides a function of survival probabilities, u, which describes the distortion factor applied by g at each u level. The quotient Q_g is a quantifier of the *local risk tolerance* of the agent at any point. The quotient value represents the relative risk attitude of the decision maker compared to that of an agent with a risk neutral attitude who is confident of the survival probability. An agent is risk neutral, risk tolerant or risk intolerant at point u if $Q_g(u)$ is equal to, lower or higher than one, respectively.

A graphical analysis of the quotient function is proposed to investigate the risk attitude of the agent at any point in the survival distribution function when using a certain risk measure. An interesting characteristic is that the quotient function is bounded. Since the quotient function computes the ratio between the distorted survival probability and the survival probability, so $\frac{1}{u}$ is the maximum value attainable by this quotient function. In fact, the maximum risk intolerance frontier at the survival value equal to u is achieved when $Q_g(u) = \frac{1}{u}$ (upper bound). Note that Q_g takes non-negative values. The maximum local risk tolerance frontier is achieved when $Q_g(u)$ is equal to zero (lower bound). In addition, when the agent does not distort the survival probabilities, $Q_g(u)$ takes value equal to 1 (local risk neutrality line).

In Figure 5.5 bounds of the Q_g are plotted. Upper and lower bounds are represented in the Figure 5.5 by a solid line. The local risk neutrality line is plotted by a dotted line. An agent's risk intolerance (tolerance) attitude emerges at point u when the quotient function is bigger (smaller) than one. As the quotient function is bounded, we can deduce at any distorted survival value how far the value is from the maximum risk intolerance/tolerance.

The evaluation of the local risk appetite pattern of a manager using the VaR$_\alpha$ and TVaR$_\alpha$ is investigated. In Figure 5.6 the quotient functions associated with the VaR$_\alpha$ and TVaR$_\alpha$ are displayed, Q_{ψ_α} and Q_{γ_α} respectively.

If we focus our attention on the quotient function associated with the VaR, Q_{ψ_α}, it can be seen that a radical risk attitude is implicit in the interval $[1-\alpha, 1)$, shifting to the opposite extreme in the interval $(0, 1-\alpha)$. Indeed, a maximum risk intolerance is involved in $[1-\alpha, 1)$ and a maximum risk tolerance attitude is involved in $(0, 1-\alpha)$. Some similarities are found when the quotient function associated with the TVaR is examined, Q_{γ_α}. Two ranges involving a different risk attitude are also distinguished. Maximum risk intolerance is involved in the interval $[1-\alpha, 1)$ and a constant (non-boundary) risk intolerance attitude is involved in $(0, 1-\alpha)$. In that interval, the quotient function value is farther to the maximum as closer is to zero the survival probability. Unlike the VaR$_\alpha$, an absolute risk intolerance attitude is associated with the TVaR$_\alpha$ because the quotient function is larger than one throughout the range $(0, 1)$.

Figure 5.5   Bounds of the quotient function

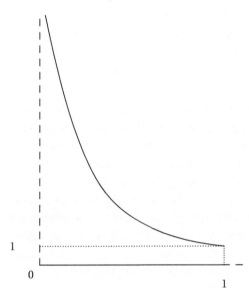

Figure 5.6   The quotient function of VaR$_\alpha$ (left) and the quotient function of TVaR$_\alpha$ (right).

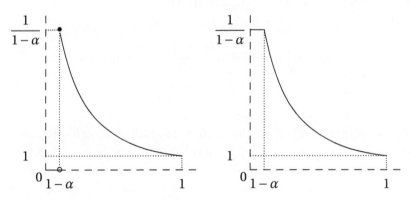

Note: Distortion functions only differ in terms of the interval $[0, 1 - \alpha)$. The quotient function of the mathematical expectation, Q_{id}, is represented by a horizontal dotted line.

The quotient function of the GlueVaR$_{\beta,\alpha}^{\omega_1,\omega_2}$ is not plotted because the particular shape for the $Q_{\kappa_{\beta,\alpha}^{\omega_1,\omega_2}}$ depends on the values of the four parameters that define the risk measure. However, as in the former two risk measures, a maximum risk intolerance is involved in the interval $[1 - \alpha, 1)$ when the quotient function of the $\text{GlueVaR}_{\beta,\alpha}^{\omega_1,\omega_2}$ is analyzed. However, more than just one attitude can be involved in the range $(0, 1 - \alpha)$. The high flexibility of $\text{GlueVaR}_{\beta,\alpha}^{\omega_1,\omega_2}$ allows multiple attitudes towards risk to be implicit in the range $(0, 1 - \alpha)$, depending on the values of the remaining three parameters, β, ω_1 and ω_2.

In short, the quotient function Q_g can be used to characterize the relative risk behavior of an agent at any point. The value of a quotient function at a particular point depends on the distortion function as well as on the original survival function. In other words, risk attitude in the quotient function is contemplated in the size of the distortion performed (the numerator) but also in the position in which this distortion is performed (the denominator). Note that the area under the quotient function provides similar information to that of the area under g, but expressed in terms of risk neutrality. Indeed, the area under the quotient function can be interpreted as the area under a weighted distortion function, where weights $(1/u)$ are given to distorted values, i.e. $g(u) \cdot \frac{1}{u}$. Following this interpretation, greater weights are assigned to distortion function values associated with lower survival values. The areas under the quotient function of VaR_α and TVaR_α are $A\left(Q_{\psi_\alpha}\right) = -\ln(1 - \alpha)$ and $A\left(Q_{\gamma_\alpha}\right) = 1 - \ln(1 - \alpha)$, respectively. Similarly, the area under the quotient function of the $\text{GlueVaR}_{\beta,\alpha}^{\omega_1,\omega_2}$ is equal to

$$A\left(Q_{\kappa_{\beta,\alpha}^{\omega_1,\omega_2}}\right) = \omega_1\left[1 + \ln\left(\frac{1-\alpha}{1-\beta}\right)\right] + \omega_2 - \ln(1 - \alpha).$$

Evaluating the area under the quotient function may be useful when analyzing the aggregate risk behavior in situations in which values of the distortion function are weighted, indicating that risk intolerance is negatively associated with the size of the survival values. Thus, the area under the quotient function can be interpreted as a weighted quantifier of the aggregate risk attitude, where an area equal to one indicates aggregate risk neutrality, an area larger than one indicates aggregate risk intolerance and an area lower than one indicates aggregate risk tolerance.

Example 5.1 (Obtaining risk attitudes of a RVaR risk measure). Taking into account the arguments presented in this chapter, the following corollaries of equivalence (4.13) proven in Section 4.3 of Chapter 4 may be stated:

· The aggregate risk attitude of $\text{RVaR}_{\alpha,\beta}$ can be obtained as the area under the distortion function plotted in Figure 4.1:

$$\frac{2-(a+b)-(1-a)}{2}+1-(2-(a+b))=\frac{1-b+2(a+b)-2}{2}$$

$$=\frac{2a+b-1}{2}$$

$$=\frac{2-2\alpha-\beta}{2} \qquad (5.1)$$

· The local risk attitude of $\text{RVaR}_{\alpha,\beta}$ is given by the following quotient function:

$$Q_{\text{RVaR}}(u) = \begin{cases} 0 & \text{if } u \in [0,\alpha] \\ \dfrac{u-\alpha}{u\beta} & \text{if } u \in (\alpha,\alpha+\beta] \\ \dfrac{1}{u} & \text{if } u \in (\alpha+\beta,1] \end{cases} \qquad (5.2)$$

A numerical illustration of the results listed before is provided. Let us evaluate a $\text{RVaR}_{0.1\%,5\%}$ risk measure. It combines VaR at the 99.9% and TVaR at the 95%. Parameters are $\alpha = 0.1\%$ and $\beta = 5\%$. From expression (5.1) the aggregate risk behavior of $\text{RVaR}_{0.1\%,5\%}$ is $\frac{2-0.2\%-5\%}{2} = \frac{194.8\%}{2} = 97.4\%$. From expression (5.2), the specific risk attitude of $\text{RVaR}_{0.1\%,5\%}$ is described by the following quotient function:

$$Q_{\text{RVaR}}(u) = \begin{cases} 0 & \text{if } u \in [0,0.1\%] \\ \dfrac{1000u-1}{50u} & \text{if } u \in (0.1\%,5.1\%] \\ \dfrac{1}{u} & \text{if } u \in (5.1\%,1] \end{cases} \qquad (5.3)$$

The equivalent GlueVaR risk measure to $\text{RVaR}_{0.1\%,5\%}$ is the one with parameters $a = 99.9\%$, $a+b-1 = 99.9\% + 95\% - 1 = 94.9\%$, $h_1 = 0$ and $h_2 = 1$. In other words,

$$\text{RVaR}_{0.1\%,5\%} = \text{GlueVaR}^{0,1}_{99.9\%,94.9\%}.$$

Given that a general expression for the overall or aggregate risk attitude behind a $\text{GlueVaR}^{\hat{h}_1,\hat{h}_2}_{\hat{\beta},\hat{\alpha}}$ risk measure is the following

$$\hat{\omega}_1\left(\frac{1+\hat{\beta}-2\hat{\alpha}}{2}\right)+\hat{\omega}_2\left(\frac{1-\hat{\alpha}}{2}\right)+\hat{\alpha}$$

let us check if, using this formula for GlueVaR$_{99.9\%,94.9\%}^{0,1}$ the 97.4% is re-covered. From expressions (4.9):

$$\widehat{a} = a + b - 1 = 94.9\%$$
$$\widehat{\beta} = a = 99.9\%$$
$$\widehat{\omega}_1 = \omega_1 = -\frac{1-a}{1-b} = -\frac{0.1\%}{5\%} = -\frac{2}{100} \qquad (5.4)$$
$$\widehat{\omega}_2 = \omega_2 = \frac{2-(a+b)}{1-b} = \frac{194.9\%}{5\%} = \frac{194.9}{5}.$$

Then

$$-\frac{2}{100}\left(\frac{1+99.9\%-2\cdot94.9\%}{2}\right) + \frac{5.1\%}{5\%}\left(\frac{1-94.9\%}{2}\right) + 94.9\%$$

$$-\frac{2}{100}\left(\frac{10.1\%}{2}\right) + \frac{5.1}{5}\left(\frac{5.1\%}{2}\right) + 94.9\%$$

$$-0.101\% + 2.601\% + 94.9\% = 2.5\% + 94.9\% = 97.4\%.$$

5.2 Application of risk assessment in a scenario involving catastrophic losses

This section illustrates how the above findings can be applied in character-izing underlying risk attitudes. It is devised to highlight situations in which the implicit risk attitude linked to the VaR is unable to detect changes in potential catastrophic losses. We argue that the use of equivalent GlueVaR risk measures can be helpful in overcoming this drawback.

Suppose that the VaR with a confidence level $\alpha = 99.5\%$ is required to as-sess the regulatory capital under some regulatory framework. Note that the selection of the confidence level involves a trade-off between protection and competitiveness. The level of the protection could be reduced with low con-fidence levels. An increase in the confidence levels could involve higher eco-nomic reserves and, therefore, the protection would rise; however, this could also affect the competitiveness.

Risk managers may dislike using the VaR as a risk measure, because of the lack of risk-based information it provides on catastrophic losses. Indeed, two firms with marked differences in the sum of their potential losses in ad-verse scenarios may report the same risk value, even though they are not exposed to the same level of risk. As such, their disparities would go un-observed by decision makers. Moreover, the lack of subadditivity may well constitute another drawback. Alternatives to $\text{VaR}_{99.5\%}$ that take into account catastrophic losses can be considered by risk managers. Traditional approaches frequently lead to severely higher economic reserves. Managers need to find a risk measure that generates similar economic reserves than $\text{VaR}_{99.5\%}$ for the overall risk faced by the insurance company and, additionally, they would like that the alternative risk measure provides risk-based information on catastrophic losses and that, hopefully, it satisfies appealing subadditivity properties.

5.2.1   Calibration of GlueVaR parameters

Our goal is to find the set of GlueVaR risk measures that return the same risk value that the $\text{VaR}_{99.5\%}$ in a particular context. So, we need to find the parameter values that define the $\text{GlueVaR}_{\beta,\alpha}^{\omega_1,\omega_2}$ risk measures. All the steps required in calibrating GlueVaR risk measures are described here. The criterion followed in the calibration procedure is the need to obtain the same risk measure value with the GlueVaR risk measures as the one obtained with the $\text{VaR}_{99.5\%}$. Moreover, the selection of the risk measure is restricted to the subfamily of GlueVaR candidates that may satisfy that their distortion function is concave in $[0, 1 - \alpha)$. The strategy for calibrating the parameters is as follows:

· Minimum and maximum admissible values of the α and β confidence levels have to be determined, $\alpha_{\min}$ and $\beta_{\max}$.

· Let us assume that Z random variable represents the overall risk. A set of $d \times d$ constrained optimization problems is defined at this step:

$$P_{i,j}: \quad \min_{\omega_1,\omega_2} |\text{GlueVaR}_{\beta_j,\alpha_i}^{\omega_1,\omega_2}(Z) - \text{VaR}_{99.5\%}(Z)|,$$

$$\text{subject to} \quad \begin{cases} 0 \leqslant \omega_1 \leqslant 1, \\ 0 \leqslant \omega_2, \\ \omega_1 + \omega_2 \leqslant 1 \end{cases}$$

where $i, j = 1, \dots, d$, $\alpha_i = \alpha_{\min} + \dfrac{i-1}{d-1}(\beta_{\max} - \alpha_{\min})$ and $\beta_j = \alpha_i + \dfrac{j-1}{d-1}(\beta_{\max} - \alpha_i)$. Flexibility rises with the number of partitions d, as do computational costs. Constraints are fixed to guarantee that the distortion function of the GlueVaR is concave in $[0, 1 - \alpha_i)$.

· An optimization algorithm should be used to solve this set of problems. If P_{i^*,j^*} represents the problem for which the minimum value of the objective function is reached and (ω_1^*, ω_2^*) is the associated solution, then a GlueVaR$^{\omega_1^*,\omega_2^*}_{\beta_{j*},\alpha_{i*}}$ is found with its distortion function concave in $[0, 1 - \alpha_{i*})$ and gives similar risk values to those obtained with VaR$_{99.5\%}$ when applied to the overall risk of the company. $P_{i,j}$ problems may not have solutions. Were this to be the case, then the optimization criteria would have to be revised, including a lower $\alpha_{\min}$, a higher $\beta_{\max}$ and/or a larger d.

· More than one GlueVaR solution is frequently found. Alternative combinations of parameter values return the same objective function value, or a value that differs insignificantly. In this situation, solutions could be ranked in accordance with the underlying risk attitude involved. Here, we propose ranking the solutions based on the value of the area under the distortion function associated with each optimal risk measure. With this goal in mind, degrees of orness are computed for (multiple) optimal GlueVaR$^{\omega_1^*,\omega_2^*}_{\beta_{j*},\alpha_{i*}}$ solutions. Two particular GlueVaR risk measures among the set of solutions are of special interest:

Lower-limit solution. Selection of the GlueVaR risk measure with the associated minimum area under the distortion function;

Upper-limit solution. Selection of the GlueVaR risk measure with the associated maximum area under the distortion function.

In other words, boundaries of the area size under distortion functions are detected. Optimal GlueVaR risk measures linked to boundaries reflect the extreme risk attitudes of agents when the random variable Z is analyzed.

5.2.2 Data and Results

We are going to use the dataset used in previous chapters. It contains X_1, X_2 and X_3. Total claim costs are the sum of the three random variables, $Z = X_1 + X_2 + X_3$. So the aggregate risk faced by the insurer is the sum of the three random variables X_i, $i = 1, 2, 3$. We assume that the insurer uses the VaR$_{99.5\%}$ as its risk measure.

Before dealing with the calibration of the GlueVaR risk measures, we first compute the VaR$_{99.5\%}(Z)$ and its associated area under its distortion function. The risk measure value is equal to VaR$_{99.5\%}(Z) = 51.05$ and the area under its distortion function is equal to 0.995. Let us now focus on the strategy used to calibrate the GlueVaR parameters. The following steps are performed to obtain GlueVaR risk measures that are comparable to the VaR$_{99.5\%}(Z)$:

a) the minimum and maximum values of confidence levels are fixed at 90% and 99.9%, i.e. $\alpha_{\min} = 90\%$ and $\beta_{\max} = 99.9\%$;

b) the number of partitions is stipulated in $d = 25$, so we deal with 625 optimization problems;

c) the empirical distribution function of total claim costs is used for the risk quantification, and, finally;

d) the outcome choice of the GlueVaR solutions are obtained using con-strOptim function from rootSolve library in R.

A more complex calibration problem involving a modified random variable including catastrophic losses can be found in Belles-Sampera *et al.* [2016c]. We obtained a set of optimal GlueVaR risk measures that give the same risk value as the VaR$_{99.5\%}$ in this specific context. Thus, 192 optimal solutions were found. Once a set of GlueVaR risk measures has been obtained as feasible solutions, the areas under the distortion functions linked to each Glue-VaR were computed to characterize the respective underlying aggregated risk attitude. The boundary values and the associated GlueVaR risk measures were identified. We should emphasize that the maximum area was equal to the area of the VaR$_{99.5\%}$. In fact, the optimal GlueVaR$_{\beta,\alpha}^{\omega_1,\omega_2}$ solution with the highest area size was the GlueVaR with parameters $\alpha = 99.5\%$, $\beta = 99.9\%$ and $\omega_1 = \omega_2 = 0$, and it holds that GlueVaR$_{99.9\%,99.5\%}^{0,0}$ = VaR$_{99.5\%}$ (see expression (3.4)). In other words, given a certain risk value, the VaR$_\alpha$ is the GlueVaR risk measure that presents the highest area under the associated distortion function of all the GlueVaR risk measures that return this value. Recall that the distortion function associated with the VaR$_\alpha$ assigns one to survival values higher than $(1 - \alpha)$ and zero to the rest.

The minimum area under the distortion function and the associated Glue-VaR risk measure for the original dataset are reported in Table 5.1. Information about the underlying aggregate risk attitude of the agent can be inferred from the minimum area. Table 5.1 shows that, for this dataset, there exists an optimal GlueVaR risk measure for which the area of the associated distortion function is approximately 0.949. Thus, this GlueVaR risk measure gives the same value as that given by VaR$_{99.5\%}$ when applied to Z, but, in aggregate terms, it involves a more moderate distortion of the original survival distribution function and, consequently, less aggregate risk intolerance.

The area under the distortion function should be complemented with the examination of the quotient function which allows the relative risk attitude at any point of the survival distribution to be analyzed. The quotient functions of risk measures associated with boundary areas in both scenarios are examined. All the quotient functions analyzed are located in the upper risk-

Table 5.1   Optimal GlueVaR risk measure

	Original dataset
α	0.900
β	0.999
ω_1	0.483
ω_2	$1.035 \cdot 10^{-6}$
ω_3	0.516
Area under the distortion function	0.949

Note: Parameter values of the associated GlueVaR risk measure equivalent to $\text{VaR}_{99.5\%}$ and minimum area under the distortion function.

tolerance frontier in the range $[0.10, 1)$. For ease of comparison, the quotient functions are rescaled and their left-tails are shown only in the range $[0, 0.10]$ in Figure 5.7.

Notable differences can be observed in the relative risk attitudes locally implicit in the left-tail of the quotient functions. Let us first examine the quotient function of the GlueVaR risk measure that presents the maximum degree of orness (left), which is the same quotient function associated with the $\text{VaR}_{99.5\%}$. The agent is most risk intolerant at any point of the interval $[0.5\%, 1)$ and maximum risk tolerant at $(0, 0.5\%)$. This means, the quotient function is located in the upper frontier at $[0.5\%, 1)$ and in the lower frontier at $(0, 0.5\%)$. When the GlueVaR risk measure that presents the minimum area is analyzed (right), the patterns of the left-tails of the quotient functions are undoubtedly different. An interesting finding is that the $Q_g(u)$ is not located within the boundaries at any point of the interval $(0, 0.10)$. This means, the risk intolerant attitude is not maximized in the range $[0.5\%, 0.10)$ but, on the contrary, the agent is more risk intolerant to catastrophic losses at $(0, 0.5\%)$ than when using $\text{VaR}_{99.5\%}$.

Figure 5.7   Quotient functions of optimal solutions

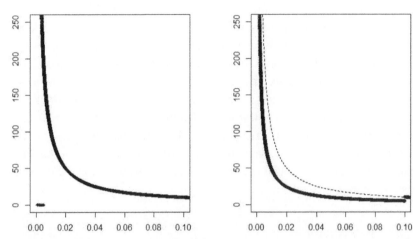

Note: Maximum (left) and minimum (right) areas under distortion functions of optimal GlueVaR risk measures. Dashed curve indicates the upper-bound quotient function curve, i.e. $\frac{1}{u}$ for all $0 \leqslant u \leqslant 1$.

5.3   GlueVaR to reflect risk attitudes

Distortion risk measures are widely used for assessing risk in a range of different contexts. As we have seen, the risk value obtained from such risk measures depends basically on the characteristics of the random variable, which are captured by the survival distribution function, and the associated distortion function. These two elements can be disaggregated and, here, our attention has focused on an analysis of the distortion function, which can be understood as a weighting function of survival probabilities. Thus, any risk attitude implicit in a distortion risk measure is to some extent attached to its distortion function.

The analysis of the risk attitude implicit in the Value at Risk illustrates that it is not sensitive to changes involving riskier scenarios. The reason for this is that the risk measure presents two extreme risk attitudes, i.e. maximum risk resistance in $[1-\alpha,1)$ and maximum risk intolerance in $(0,1-\alpha)$. Here, we have shown that additional risk information may be obtained using comparable GlueVaR risk measures that are calibrated to report the same risk value as that of the VaR_{α}. The calibration procedure of GlueVaR parameters was not the primary focus of this chapter and it was not our intention to cover all the possible calibration criteria. However, two final remarks are worth recording. First, the procedure proposed depends necessarily on the risk measure of reference and also on the random variable. As such, the set of comparable GlueVaR risk measures differs when the random variable changes. This is not an unbridgeable drawback when requesting to the supervisory authorities authorization for changing the risk measure to a Glue-VaR one, if decision makers are able to justify the GlueVaR selection process. For example, these measures may be used to analyze variations from one year to next in the implicit risk attitude of boundary cases when the VaR_α is applied to assess the annual risk. Second, the VaR_α was chosen as the risk measure of reference because of its application in practice, but the calibration strategy of the GlueVaR risk measures could easily be adapted to other risk measurement problems.

5.4 Exercises

1. Compare the area under the distortion function of the GlueVaR$_{85\%,50\%}^{11/30,2/3}$, GlueVaR$_{85\%,50\%}^{0,1}$ and the GlueVaR$_{85\%,50\%}^{1/20,1/8}$. What do you can say in terms of aggregate risk attitude associated to these risk measures?

   Hint: The heights (h_1, h_2) equal to $(11/30, 2/3)$, $(0, 1)$, and $(1/20, 1/8)$ correspond to $(\omega_1 = 1/3, \omega_2 = 1/3)$, $(\omega_1 = -1/9, \omega_2 = 10/9)$ and $(\omega_1 = 1/24, \omega_2 = 1/12)$, respectively.

2. Plot the quotient functions of previous GlueVaR risk measures. Discuss what additional information (if there are) in terms of local risk attitude is provided when the quotient function of these risk measures is analyzed.

3. Compute the area under the distortion functions of the RVaR$_{1\%,5\%}$ and RVaR$_{5\%,1\%}$.

   · What do you can say in terms of aggregate risk attitude associated to these risk measures?
   · Discuss their quotient functions in terms of the implicit local risk attitude.

4. Analyze the area under the distortion function and the quotient function of the Wang-Transform risk measure [Wang, 2002]. Discuss the relationship between α and the underlying risk attitude.

   Hint: The distortion function of the Wang-Transform risk measure is defined as $g(u) = \Phi[\Phi^{-1}(u) - \lambda]$, where $u = S(x)$ and $\lambda = \Phi^{-1}(\alpha)$ with the security level α.

PART II

CAPITAL ALLOCATION PROBLEMS

6 An overview on capital allocation problems

Capital allocation problems of insurance and financial institutions arise when a management unit must distribute an amount of resources among different business units. These resources may be the aggregate cost faced by the company, its solvency capital requirement or the total variable economic compensation to be shared across business units, among other examples. This kind of problems are frequent and relevant from an Enterprise Risk Management (ERM) perspective, mainly if the risk that each business unit faces is, somehow, taken into account for the final allocation. Sometimes the capital allocation is merely notional, as pointed out in Dhaene *et al.* [2012b]. This does not diminish the importance of studying these problems at all. The allocation information may be useful to conduct different business analyses in order to improve the risk management of the company.

Main concepts and notations regarding capital allocation problems are introduced in the next section. These are the building blocks on which the rest of the discussion is based and represent a necessary starting point to go further in next chapters. The overview on capital allocation problems is completed with a description of some particularly interesting solutions and with a list of properties that particular solutions to these problems may satisfy.

6.1 Main concepts and notation

In general terms, a capital allocation problem may be understood in the following way:

"An amount $K > 0$ of monetary units has to be distributed across $n \in \mathbb{N}$ agents, and the allocation must be a *full allocation*."

Described in such a way, capital allocation problems can be understood as *disaggregation problems*. Several comments must be made in relation to capital allocation problems. First of all, on the risk management framework in which this kind of problems arises. These problems are strongly related to the fact that risk managers from the insurance and banking industries must determine, at different levels of granularity, the contributions of *agents* to the risk-based regulatory capital required to companies. In that sense, the concept of agent must be understood in a broad way: it may be a commercial agent, a business unit, a branch of the overall business or even a particular guarantee included in a set of contracts. Nonetheless, it has to be noted that similar risk management problems are faced by asset management firms when planning investment strategies or when assessing performance of their investment portfolios. In such contexts it is more usual to refer to these problems as *portfolio risk attribution or risk budgeting problems* [see, for instance, Grégoire, 2007; Rahl, 2012].

Secondly, it is important to list the main elements that play a role in a capital allocation problem. Capital allocation problems may be described by means of the following elements:

· The capital $K > 0$ to be distributed;

· The agents, indexed by $i = 1, \ldots, n$;

· Random variables linked to each agent, $\{X_i\}_{i=1,\ldots,n}$;

· Functions f_i, $i = 1, \ldots, n$, used to simplify the information provided by each X_i;

· A distribution criterion;

· Capitals K_i, $i = 1, \ldots, n$, assigned to each agent as a solution to the problem;

· The goal that is pursued with the allocation. Some examples are *cost of risk* allocation, *reward to riskless* allocation or *reward on risk and return* (*risk&return*) allocation.

In particular, a solution of a capital allocation problem is the set of n capitals $\{K_i\}_{i=1,\ldots,n}$ allocated to each agent, where capital K_i is the amount of capital assigned to the ith agent. It is usually required that the solution satisfies the *full allocation* property. It happens when the set of capitals adds up to K, that is, $\sum_{i=1}^{n} K_i = K$. The capital amount assigned to the ith agent K_i is related to the risk X_i faced by that agent. Random variables X_i, $i = 1, \ldots, n$, are frequently representing ith agent's losses.

A solution to a capital allocation problem is called a capital allocation principle. One of the fundamental elements characterizing a capital allocation principle is the distribution criterion that drives the allocation. Proportional allocation criteria are such that each capital K_i, $i = 1,\ldots,n$, may be expressed as the product of capital K times a proportion of the form

$$\frac{f_i(X_i)}{\sum\limits_{j=1}^{n} f_j(X_j)},$$

where f_i functions simplify all the information provided by X_i. Therefore, the general expression for a proportional allocation principle is

$$K_i = K \cdot \frac{f_i(X_i)}{\sum\limits_{j=1}^{n} f_j(X_j)}, \quad i = 1,\ldots,n. \tag{6.1}$$

Frequently, functions f_i are risk measures or partial contributions to the value that a risk measure assigns to the whole random loss understood as $S = \sum_{j=1}^{n} X_j$. If f_i is a risk measure ρ, the proportional allocation principle is classified as a *stand-alone* proportional allocation principle. On the other hand, when dealing with $\{f_i\}_{i=1,\ldots,n}$ which represent partial contributions to $\rho(S)$ for a given risk measure ρ, the proportional allocation principle is based on *marginal or partial contributions*. The name is inherited by the fact that expression $\rho(S) = \sum_{j=1}^{n} f_j(X_j)$ holds. In such those cases, notation $f_i(X_i) = \rho(X_i \mid S)$ is going to be used and, therefore, the general expression for proportional allocation principles based on partial contributions is

$$K_i = K \cdot \frac{\rho(X_i \mid S)}{\rho(S)}, \quad i = 1,\ldots,n. \tag{6.2}$$

Among proportional capital allocation principles, the main difference between stand-alone principles and the ones based on partial contributions is related to diversification effects. Stand-alone principles do not take into account neither benefits nor penalizations on risk of each ith agent due to the fact that the agent belongs to a set of agents, while principles based on partial contributions do. That is, stand-alone principles do not take into account dependencies between risks and partial contributions based principles take into account that risks are interconnected.

Non-proportional allocation principles are such that an expression like (6.1) for each of the assigned capitals K_i, $i = 1,\ldots,n$, cannot be achieved. An example of non-proportional principle is the *excess based allocation principle* shown in Section 6.3.3.

A significant number of principles can be included in the framework provided by Dhaene *et al.* [2012b]. For instance, when using the so-called *quadratic optimization criterion*, principles like

$$K_i = \rho_i(X_i) + v_i \cdot \left[K - \sum_{j=1}^{n} \rho_j(X_j) \right], \qquad (6.3)$$

where ρ_i, $i = 1, \ldots, n$, are risk measures and v_i are weights such that $\sum_{j=1}^{n} v_j$ = 1. If all v_i are equal to $\rho_i(X_i) / \left(\sum_{j=1}^{n} \rho_j(X_j) \right)$, then it is a proportional allocation principle. To obtain non-proportional allocation principles, at least one of the v_i, say v_{i_0}, must be not equal to $\rho_i(X_i) / \left(\sum_{j=1}^{n} \rho_j(X_j) \right)$. In other words, there must exist an $i_0 \in \{1, \ldots, n\}$ such that

$$v_{i_0} \neq \frac{\rho_{i_0}(X_{i_0})}{\sum_{j=1}^{n} \rho_j(X_j)} .$$

Last but not least, a major issue is the goal pursued with the allocation. We here propose three different goals: *cost of risk*, *reward to riskless* and *reward on risk and return*. Other alternative goals may be considered and they will depend on the opinion of decision makers (risk managers, regulators, etc.). The aim of a capital allocation problem with a *cost of risk* goal is to distribute the cost among the agents by taking into account some measure of the risk faced by each one of them. An example of such a *cost of risk* allocation is the disaggregation of the Solvency Capital Requirement (SCR) of the whole business of an European insurance company under the Solvency II regime among its lines of business.

Assume that a management team wants to stimulate a risk averse attitude among the business units it has in charge, this management team may adopt a compensation scheme based on the following idea: the riskier the business unit is, the lesser the reward it receives. In such a situation, a capital allocation problem with a *reward to riskless* objective is conducted. This kind of problems rarely appears in practice. But, if we try to think in an example of such a capital allocation problem, it could appear when there is the request of notionally distributing the contribution of each agent to the overall diversification benefit, where only there is information about a final *cost of risk* allocation and the overall diversification benefit. That is, where there is not information about each individual diversification benefit.

A much more frequent problem faced by managers in practice is to allocate capital under a *reward on risk and return* criterion, in order to better reward those agents whose trade-off between return obtained and risk faced is higher. In this context, a return-on-risk measure seems to be the natural choice of functions $\{f_i\}_{i=1,\ldots,n}$ in order to assign rewards under the *reward on risk and return* perspective. In next sections some examples related to this type of allocation are going to be provided.

A principle is denoted in this book by $\vec{K} = (K_1, K_2, \ldots, K_n)$. An abuse of notation is made because K is used both to denote the vector $\vec{K}$ whose components are K_i and the capital to be distributed among agents. Given an (absolute) capital allocation principle $\vec{K}$ with $K = \sum_{j=1}^{n} K_j$, its relative counterpart is defined as the n dimensional vector $\vec{x}$, whose components are $x_i = K_i/K$ and satisfy that $\sum_{j=1}^{n} x_j = 1$. If there is no room for confusion, upper-case letters mean absolute principles while lower-case letters mean relative ones. This notation is used in next chapters.

6.2 Properties of capital allocation principles

As in the case of risk measures, capital allocations have been often studied from an axiomatic point of view. Denault [2001] defines a set of axioms that capital allocations should satisfy. Allocations satisfying some of these axioms[1] were called *coherent* allocations therein, in line with the idea of *coherent* risk measures previously introduced by Artzner *et al.* [1999]. Let X_i, $i = 1, \ldots, n$, be the set of risks and $S = X_1 + \cdots + X_n$ their sum. Consider a risk measure $\rho(S)$ and capital allocation principles for which $K = \rho(S)$ and K_i, $i = 1, \ldots, n$ are partial contributions $K_i = \rho(X_i \mid S)$ such that $\rho(S) = \sum_{i=1}^{n} \rho(X_i \mid S)$. The properties that those capital allocation principles should satisfy are:

· **Consistency** (or riskless allocation)
  The capital allocated to a risk that has no uncertainty is equal to the certain risk.
  If $X_i = k$ for any constant $k \in \mathbb{R}$ then $K_i = \rho(X_i \mid S) = k$.

· **Full allocation**
  The capital for the overall risk is split into capitals for all individual risks, that is

$$\rho(a_1 X_1 + \cdots + a_n X_n) = \sum_{i=1}^{n} \rho(a_i X_i \mid S), \quad a_i \in \mathbb{R}^+.$$

---

[1] No undercut, symmetry and riskless allocation (or consistency).

If ρ satisfies the positive homogeneity property, then this is equivalent to

$$\rho(a_1 X_1 + \cdots + a_n X_n) = \sum_{i=1}^{n} a_i \rho(X_i \mid S).$$

Notice that for $a_i = 1$, for all $i = 1, \ldots, n$,

$$\rho\left(\sum_{i=1}^{n} X_i\right) = \sum_{i=1}^{n} \rho(X_i \mid S).$$

· **No undercut**
  The capital allocation for any decomposition of total risk undercut is not higher than the capital amount that it would be allocated as a separated portfolio.
  For any subset of N, $A \subseteq N$, where $N = \{1, \ldots, n\}$, it is satisfied that

$$\sum_{i \in A} K_i = \sum_{i \in A} \rho(X_i \mid S) \leq \rho\left(\sum_{i \in A} X_i\right).$$

· **No diversification**
  If there are not diversification benefits for the agents when considered together in terms of risk (i.e. if $\sum_{i=1}^{n} \rho(X_i) = \rho(S)$) then the capital allocation principle becomes really simple: the stand-alone risk of each agent is the amount allocated to it. If $\sum_{i=1}^{n} \rho(X_i) = \rho(S)$ then $K_i = \rho(X_i)$ for all $i = 1, \ldots, n$.

· **Symmetry**
  For two identical risks, $X_i = X_j$, $i \neq j$, the allocated capital must be the same $\rho(X_i \mid S) = \rho(X_j \mid S)$.

· **Continuity**
  Infinitesimal variations on the whole risk have no impact on risk allocations,
$$\lim_{h \to 0} \rho(X_i \mid S + h) = \rho(X_i \mid S).$$

This is not a complete list of properties. Other properties as translation invariance, scale invariance or monotonicity with respect to a concordance ordering are often asked to capital allocation principles. The interested reader is referred, for instance, to van Gulick *et al.* [2012].

6.3   Review of some principles

A collection of particular principles is included in this section. Three partial contribution based capital allocation principles are defined and one non-proportional capital allocation principle. This section does not pursue to be a deep review of principles found in the literature. The principles discussed in this section have been selected for exposition purposes. The attention has been paid to specific issues of each capital allocation principle, so a non-homogeneous extension is found in the discussion of each principle.

6.3.1   The gradient allocation principle

This principle is also known as Euler allocation principle [McNeil *et al.*, 2005] or, from a game-theoretic perspective, as Aumann-Shapley allocation principle [Denault, 2001]. According to Tasche [1999, 2004, 2007] capital allocation principles based on the gradient are the most appropriate allocation principles to deal with risk adjusted returns. Since *reward on risk and return* allocations could be specially useful in sound ERM systems, the key elements of the gradient allocation principle and its usefulness as *reward on risk and return* allocations are discussed in detail in this section.

The basic idea that must be remarked is that the gradient allocation principle takes advantage of the Euler's theorem on homogeneous functions applied to positively homogeneous risk measures. The definition of homogeneous functions and the Euler's theorem are as follows.

Definition 6.1 (Homogeneous function of degree r). Let f be a function from $\mathbb{R}^n$ to $\mathbb{R}$, $n > 0$.

$$f \text{ is homogeneous of degree } r \iff \forall \lambda \in \mathbb{R}, \ f(\lambda \cdot \vec{u}) = \lambda^r \cdot f(\vec{u}).$$

Theorem 6.1 (Euler's theorem on homogeneous functions). *Let $f : \mathbb{R}^n \to \mathbb{R}$ be a differentiable function on $\mathbb{R}^n$. Then,*

$$f \text{ is an homogeneous function of degree } r \iff \sum_{i=1}^{n} u_i \cdot \frac{\partial f}{\partial u_i}(\vec{u}) = r \cdot f(\vec{u}).$$

It has to be noted that a differentiable function f defined from $\mathbb{R}^n$ to $\mathbb{R}$ has a gradient equal to $\nabla f(\vec{u}) = \left(\frac{\partial f}{\partial u_1}(\vec{u}), \frac{\partial f}{\partial u_2}(\vec{u}), \ldots, \frac{\partial f}{\partial u_n}(\vec{u}) \right)$ and, therefore, the right-hand side of the equivalence in Theorem 6.1 can be also written as $\langle \vec{u}, \nabla f(\vec{u}) \rangle = r \cdot f(\vec{u})$, where $\langle \ , \ \rangle$ stands for the interior product in $\mathbb{R}^n$.

Consider now a positively homogeneous risk measure ρ. This means that $\rho(\lambda \cdot X) = \lambda \cdot \rho(X)$ for all $\lambda \geqslant 0$ and for all $X \in \Gamma$, as we have seen in Table 1.2 of Chapter 1. Now, given a random vector $\vec{X} = (X_1, X_2, \ldots, X_n) \in \Gamma^n$, consider the following function $f_{\vec{X}}$ as well:

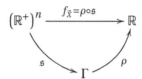

$$\vec{u} \longmapsto \mathfrak{s}(\vec{u}) = \sum_{i=1}^{n} u_i X_i \longmapsto \rho(\mathfrak{s}(\vec{u})) = \rho\left(\sum_{i=1}^{n} u_i X_i\right) = f_{\vec{X}}(\vec{u}) \qquad (6.4)$$

Taking into account Definition 6.1 restricted to $(\mathbb{R}^+)^n$, considering that ρ is a positively homogeneous risk measure, and noting that $\sum_{i=1}^{n} u_i X_i \in \Gamma$ for all $\vec{u} \in (\mathbb{R}^+)^n$ if $\vec{X} \in \Gamma^n$, then it is deduced that $f_{\vec{X}}$ is an *homogeneous function of degree* $r = 1$. In such a case, applying Theorem 6.1 the following expression holds:

$$f_{\vec{X}}(\vec{u}) = \sum_{i=1}^{n} u_i \cdot \frac{\partial f_{\vec{X}}}{\partial u_i}(\vec{u}) = \langle \vec{u}, \nabla f_{\vec{X}}(\vec{u}) \rangle. \qquad (6.5)$$

If $\vec{u} = (1, 1, \ldots, 1)$ then the sum $\sum_{i=1}^{n} u_i X_i$ is the sum of all the components of the random vector $\vec{X}$. From this point forward, this sum is denoted as S, so $S = \sum_{i=1}^{n} X_i$. If the following simplified notation is used

$$\frac{\partial \rho}{\partial u_i}(S) = \frac{\partial f_{\vec{X}}}{\partial u_i}(\vec{u})_{|\vec{u}=(1,1,\ldots,1)},$$

then expression (6.5) becomes

$$\rho(S) = \sum_{i=1}^{n} \frac{\partial \rho}{\partial u_i}(S), \qquad (6.6)$$

which is the formula usually related to the underlying idea of the Euler allocation principle.

Example 6.1. Let W_1 and W_2 be two independent random variables identically distributed as standard Normal distributions. Consider $X_1 = W_1$ and $X_2 = \frac{1}{2} \cdot W_1 + \frac{\sqrt{3}}{2} \cdot W_2$. Obviously, X_1 is distributed as a standard Normal distribution and it is easy to check that X_2 too, although X_1 and X_2 are not independent but there is a linear correlation of 50% between them. Consider now two positive deterministic returns $r_1 > 0$ and $r_2 > 0$ and two assets whose random returns can be represented by $Y_1 = r_1 + X_1$ and $Y_2 = r_2 + X_2$. Investing in $u_1 \geqslant 0$ units of the first asset and in $u_2 \geqslant 0$ units of the second one a portfolio with return $\mathfrak{r}(\vec{u}) = u_1 \cdot Y_1 + u_2 \cdot Y_2$ is obtained. By construction, the return of this portfolio is Normally distributed, with mean equal to $u_1 \cdot r_1 + u_2 \cdot r_2$ and variance equal to

$$
\begin{aligned}
\mathbb{V}(\mathfrak{r}(\vec{u})) &= \mathbb{E}\left([\mathfrak{r}(\vec{u}) - \mathbb{E}(\mathfrak{r}(\vec{u})]^2\right) \\
&= \mathbb{E}\left(\left[(u_1 + 0.5 \cdot u_2) \cdot W_1 + \frac{\sqrt{3}}{2} \cdot u_2 \cdot W_2\right]^2\right) \\
&= \left(u_1^2 + u_1 \cdot u_2 + \frac{1}{4} \cdot u_2^2\right) \cdot \mathbb{E}(W_1^2) + \frac{3}{4} \cdot u_2^2 \cdot \mathbb{E}(W_2^2) \\
&\quad + 2 \cdot \left(u_1 + \frac{1}{2} \cdot u_2\right) \cdot \frac{\sqrt{3}}{2} \cdot u_1 \cdot u_2 \cdot \mathbb{E}(W_1 \cdot W_2) \\
&= u_1^2 + u_1 \cdot u_2 + u_2^2.
\end{aligned}
$$

Starting from an initial portfolio of u_1^0 units of the first asset and u_2^0 units of the second one, we are interested in allocating the risk faced by this portfolio (measured with the VaR risk measure at some confidence level) using the gradient allocation principle. Is this possible?

First thing to be noticed is that positive values of returns $\mathfrak{r}(\vec{u})$ are profits and not losses. This is important in order to calculate the risk faced by the portfolio, because if $\alpha \in (0, 1)$ is the chosen confidence level then we are going to compute $\rho(\mathfrak{s}(\vec{u})) = \text{VaR}_\alpha(-\mathfrak{r}(\vec{u}))$ or, in other words, the loss function that we are going to consider is $\mathfrak{s}(\vec{u}) = -\mathfrak{r}(\vec{u})$ (recall the discussion with respect to the 'liability' or the 'asset' side perspectives provided in Section 1.2.1). The second remark is more subtle and it is related to ensure that $\rho(\mathfrak{s}(\vec{u}))$ is an homogeneous function of degree 1 on $\mathbb{R}^2$, because this is a necessary condition to be allowed to apply the Euler's Theorem. In this case, there is no problem with $\rho(\mathfrak{s}(\vec{u}))$, because $\rho = \text{VaR}_\alpha$ is a positively homogeneous risk measure and $\mathfrak{s}(\vec{u}) = -u_1 \cdot Y_1 - u_2 \cdot Y_2$ is linear in u_1 and u_2, so homogeneous of degree 1. But note that, for instance, if we change the actual Y_1 by $Y_1 = \log(u_1 + \frac{1}{2}) + X_1$ then the associated $\mathfrak{s}(\vec{u})$ is not homogeneous of degree 1 and conditions to successfully apply the gradient allocation principle are not satisfied.

Following the notation introduced in expression (6.4) let us compute $f_{\vec{Y}}(\vec{u}) = \text{VaR}_\alpha(\mathfrak{s}(\vec{u}))$ and its gradient $\nabla f_{\vec{Y}}(\vec{u})$. We have already shown that $\mathfrak{r}(\vec{u})$ is

Normally distributed so, recalling Table 1.3 in Chapter 1:

$$\text{VaR}_\alpha(\mathfrak{s}(\vec{u})) = -u_1 \cdot r_1 - u_2 \cdot r_2 + \Phi^{-1}(\alpha) \cdot \sqrt{u_1^2 + u_1 \cdot u_2 + u_2^2}. \quad (6.7)$$

Note that the previous expression is symmetric in u_i, $i = 1, 2$. The gradient of $\text{VaR}_\alpha(\mathfrak{s}(\vec{u}))$ is the vector with the following components

$$\frac{\partial \text{VaR}_\alpha(\mathfrak{s}(\vec{u}))}{\partial u_1} = -r_1 + \Phi^{-1}(\alpha) \cdot \frac{(2 \cdot u_1 + u_2) \cdot \sqrt{u_1^2 + u_1 \cdot u_2 + u_2^2}}{2 \cdot (u_1^2 + u_1 \cdot u_2 + u_2^2)},$$

$$\frac{\partial \text{VaR}_\alpha(\mathfrak{s}(\vec{u}))}{\partial u_2} = -r_2 + \Phi^{-1}(\alpha) \cdot \frac{(u_1 + 2 \cdot u_2) \cdot \sqrt{u_1^2 + u_1 \cdot u_2 + u_2^2}}{2 \cdot (u_1^2 + u_1 \cdot u_2 + u_2^2)}. \quad (6.8)$$

All the elements to derive the capital allocation based on the gradient principle are now available, so with respect to the portfolio consisting in u_1^0 units of the first asset and u_2^0 units of the second one and taking into account expression (6.5) the final allocation becomes the following:

$$\text{VaR}_\alpha\left(-u_1^0 \cdot Y_1 \mid -u_1^0 \cdot Y_1 - u_2^0 \cdot Y_2\right)$$

$$= -u_1^0 \cdot r_1 + \Phi^{-1}(\alpha) \cdot \frac{(2 \cdot (u_1^0)^2 + u_1^0 \cdot u_2^0) \cdot \sqrt{(u_1^0)^2 + u_1^0 \cdot u_2^0 + (u_2^0)^2}}{2 \cdot ((u_1^0)^2 + u_1^0 \cdot u_2^0 + (u_2^0)^2)},$$

$$(6.9)$$

$$\text{VaR}_\alpha\left(-u_2^0 \cdot Y_2 \mid -u_1^0 \cdot Y_1 - u_2^0 \cdot Y_2\right)$$

$$= -u_2^0 \cdot r_2 + \Phi^{-1}(\alpha) \cdot \frac{(u_1^0 \cdot u_2^0 + 2 \cdot (u_2^0)^2) \cdot \sqrt{(u_1^0)^2 + u_1^0 \cdot u_2^0 + (u_2^0)^2}}{2 \cdot ((u_1^0)^2 + u_1^0 \cdot u_2^0 + (u_2^0)^2)}.$$

Let us complete the example with some numbers, similar to those that can be found in Buch et al. [2011]. Imagine that our starting portfolio consists in the combination of $u_1^0 = 1.5$ units of the first asset and $u_2^0 = 1.7$ units of the second one, and that the deterministic returns r_1 and r_2 are $r_1 = 46.2098\%$ and $r_2 = 46.3798\%$, respectively. Additionally, let the confidence level α be equal to 99.97%, so $\Phi^{-1}(\alpha) = 3.4316$. The random loss of the portfolio has the following expression $\mathfrak{s}(\vec{u}^0) = -1.5 \cdot Y_1 - 1.7 \cdot Y_2$ and

$$\mathbb{E}(\mathfrak{s}(\vec{u}^0)) = -1.5 \cdot 46.2098\% - 1.7 \cdot 46.3798\% = -148.1605\%,$$

$$\mathbb{V}(\mathfrak{s}(\vec{u}^0)) = (-1.5)^2 + (-1.5) \cdot (-1.7) + (-1.7)^2 = 7.69, \quad (6.10)$$

$$\text{VaR}_{99.97\%}(\mathfrak{s}(\vec{u}^0)) = -148.1605\% + 3.4316 \cdot \sqrt{7.69} = 803.4554\%,$$

so a really profitable return of 148.1605% is expected (negative losses mean gains) and negative returns will not be under -803.4554% in the 99.97% of situations. How may this potential risk be allocated to the assets? One possibility is to use the gradient allocation principle as derived in expression (6.9):

$$
\begin{aligned}
\text{VaR}_{99.97\%}&(-1.5\cdot Y_1 \mid -1.5\cdot Y_1 - 1.7\cdot Y_2) \\
&= -69.3147\% + 3.4316\cdot \frac{7.05\cdot 2.7731}{2\cdot 7.69} = 366.8941\%, \text{ and} \\
\text{VaR}_{99.97\%}&(-1.7\cdot Y_2 \mid -1.5\cdot Y_1 - 1.7\cdot Y_2) \\
&= -78.8457\% + 3.4316\cdot \frac{8.33\cdot 2.7731}{2\cdot 7.69} = 436.5613\%.
\end{aligned}
\tag{6.11}
$$

Note that, as it may be expected,

$$
\begin{aligned}
\text{VaR}_{99.97\%}(\mathfrak{s}(\vec{u}^0)) = \text{VaR}_{99.97\%}&\left(-1.5\cdot Y_1 \mid \mathfrak{s}(\vec{u}^0)\right) \\
&+ \text{VaR}_{99.97\%}(-1.7\cdot Y_2 \mid \mathfrak{s}(\vec{u}^0))
\end{aligned}
$$

$$
(803.4554\% = 366.8941\% + 436.5613\%).
$$

Another way to interpret the allocation provided in expression (6.11) is that the 45.66% (366.8941%/803.4554%) of the risk is allocated to the first asset and the 54.34% of the risk is allocated to the second one.

Now, it is shown that the gradient allocation principle is the most appropriate principle to deal with *reward on risk and return*. First, we consider a particular *Return on Risk Adjusted Capital* (RORAC) measure, and some concepts and notations taken from Tasche [2007]:

Definition 6.2. The total RORAC of portfolio $S = \sum_{i=1}^n X_i$ is defined by

$$
\text{RORAC}(S) = \frac{-\mathbb{E}(S)}{\rho(S)},
$$

where ρ is a risk measure and each random variable X_i, $i = 1,\ldots,n$ is such that its positive values represent losses.

Definition 6.3. Given a portfolio $S = \sum_{i=1}^n X_i$ and a set of contributions $\rho(X_i \mid S)$, $i = 1,\ldots,n$, to the value of the risk of the portfolio measured by ρ, i.e. $\rho(S) = \sum_{i=1}^n \rho(X_i \mid S)$, the portfolio-related RORAC of each random variable X_i is defined by

$$
\text{RORAC}(X_i \mid S) = \frac{-\mathbb{E}(X_i)}{\rho(X_i \mid S)}, \quad \forall i = 1,\ldots,n.
$$

Note that, in most of the situations, numerators in Definitions 6.2 and 6.3 are positive, because the mathematical expectations of S and X_i, $i = 1,\ldots,n$, are negative: it may be assumed that ith business unit does not expect losses, so $\mathbb{E}(X_i) < 0$ due to the fact that positive values of X_i mean losses. A second remark is that the Definition 6.3 depends on both portfolio S and partial contributions to $\rho(S)$. Bearing these two previous definitions in mind, let us now present the RORAC compatibility definition provided by Tasche [2007]:

Definition 6.4 (RORAC compatible risk contributions). Risk contributions $\rho(X_i \mid S), i = 1,\ldots,n$ are RORAC compatible if there are some $\epsilon_i > 0, i = 1,\ldots,n$ such that

$$\text{RORAC}(X_i \mid S) > \text{RORAC}(S) \implies$$

$$\text{RORAC}(S + hX_i) > \text{RORAC}(S) \quad \text{for all} \quad 0 < h < \epsilon_i$$

According to the definition of RORAC compatibility, if the partial *risk and return* performance of ith agent given by Definition 6.3 is greater than the *risk and return* performance of the overall portfolio given by Definition 6.2, then the *risk and return* performance of the overall portfolio is improved by slightly increasing the position of ith agent in the portfolio. In other words, if some $\text{RORAC}(X_i \mid S)$ is greater than the $\text{RORAC}(S)$ and the contribution $\rho(X_i \mid S)$ is RORAC compatible, then the position on ith agent should be increased in order to improve the overall performance of the portfolio.

Assuming that it is possible to slightly increase the position of ith agent in the portfolio, going from X_i to $X_i \cdot (1 + h)$ with $h \in (0, \epsilon_i)$, the necessary condition expressed in Definition 6.4 can be understood as equivalent to the following one

$$\frac{\partial \text{RORAC}}{\partial u_i}(\mathfrak{s}(\vec{u}))_{|\vec{u}=(1,1,\ldots,1)} > 0, \tag{6.12}$$

simply by computing

$$\lim_{h \to 0} \frac{1}{h}\left[\text{RORAC}(S + hX_i) - \text{RORAC}(S)\right].$$

Taking advantage of expression (6.12) the RORAC compatibility of the gradient allocation principle can be proved.

Proposition 6.1. *Suppose that* $\rho(\mathfrak{s}(\vec{u}))$ *and* $\dfrac{\partial f_{\vec{X}}}{\partial u_i}(\vec{u})$ *for all* $i = 1, \ldots, n$, *are strictly positive. A gradient allocation principle* $\vec{K} \in \mathbb{R}^n$ *of the form* $K_i = K \cdot \dfrac{\rho(X_i \mid S)}{\rho(S)}$ *where risk contributions are* $\rho(X_i \mid S) = \dfrac{\partial \rho}{\partial u_i}(S)$ *for all* $i = 1, \ldots, n$, *is such that all the risk contributions are RORAC compatible.*

Proof. Let us show that expression (6.12) holds for each $i = 1, \ldots, n$:

$$
\begin{aligned}
\frac{\partial \text{RORAC}}{\partial u_i}(\mathfrak{s}(\vec{u})) &= \frac{\partial}{\partial u_i}\left[\frac{-\mathbb{E}\left(\sum_{j=1}^n u_j \cdot X_j\right)}{\rho\left(\sum_{j=1}^n u_j \cdot X_j\right)} \right] \\
&= \frac{\frac{\partial}{\partial u_i}\left[-\mathbb{E}\left(\sum_{j=1}^n u_j \cdot X_j\right)\right] \cdot \rho\left(\sum_{j=1}^n u_j \cdot X_j\right)}{\left[\rho\left(\sum_{j=1}^n u_j \cdot X_j\right)\right]^2} \\
&\quad - \frac{\left[-\mathbb{E}\left(\sum_{j=1}^n u_j \cdot X_j\right)\right] \cdot \frac{\partial}{\partial u_i}\rho\left(\sum_{j=1}^n u_j \cdot X_j\right)}{\left[\rho\left(\sum_{j=1}^n u_j \cdot X_j\right)\right]^2} \\
&= \frac{\frac{\partial}{\partial u_i}\left[-\mathbb{E}\left(\sum_{j=1}^n u_j \cdot X_j\right)\right] \cdot \rho(\mathfrak{s}(\vec{u})) - [-\mathbb{E}(\mathfrak{s}(\vec{u}))] \cdot \frac{\partial f_{\vec{X}}}{\partial u_i}(\vec{u})}{[\rho(\mathfrak{s}(\vec{u}))]^2} \\
&= \frac{-\mathbb{E}(X_i) \cdot \rho(\mathfrak{s}(\vec{u})) + [\mathbb{E}(\mathfrak{s}(\vec{u}))] \cdot \frac{\partial f_{\vec{X}}}{\partial u_i}(\vec{u})}{[\rho(\mathfrak{s}(\vec{u}))]^2}.
\end{aligned}
$$

As long as the denominator of the previous expression is always positive, then it is deduced that $\dfrac{\partial \text{RORAC}}{\partial u_i}(\mathfrak{s}(\vec{u})) > 0$ if and only if $-\mathbb{E}(X_i) \cdot \rho(\mathfrak{s}(\vec{u})) +$ $\mathbb{E}(\mathfrak{s}(\vec{u})) \cdot \dfrac{\partial f_{\vec{X}}}{\partial u_i}(\vec{u}) > 0$. Consider that both $\rho(\mathfrak{s}(\vec{u}))$ and $\dfrac{\partial f_{\vec{X}}}{\partial u_i}(\vec{u})$ are strictly positive: these conditions may usually hold, because of dealing with risk values or risk contributions of a portfolio of risky positions. But note that, in fact, these conditions have been required as hypotheses in the proposition. Being this the case, this last expression may be written as

$$
\frac{-\mathbb{E}(X_i)}{\dfrac{\partial f_{\vec{X}}}{\partial u_i}(\vec{u})} > \frac{-\mathbb{E}(\mathfrak{s}(\vec{u}))}{\rho(\mathfrak{s}(\vec{u}))}.
$$

Moreover, when restricted to $\vec{u} = (1, 1, \ldots, 1)$ this last expression provides the following information:

$$\frac{\partial \text{RORAC}}{\partial u_i}(\mathfrak{s}(\vec{u}))|_{\vec{u}=(1,1,\dots,1)} > 0, \text{ if and only if}$$

$$\frac{-\mathbb{E}(X_i)}{\dfrac{\partial \rho}{\partial u_i}(S)} > \frac{-\mathbb{E}(S)}{\rho(S)} \iff \frac{-\mathbb{E}(X_i)}{\rho(X_i \mid S)} > \frac{-\mathbb{E}(S)}{\rho(S)}$$

$$\iff \text{RORAC}(X_i \mid S) > \text{RORAC}(S). \qquad\qquad \square$$

Example 6.2. Let us continue with the example shown previously in this chapter, in order to illustrate RORAC calculations and to check that, when using the gradient allocation principle, the RORAC compatibility is satisfied. First of all, let us compute the total RORAC of the portfolio (recall expression 6.2) and the portfolio-related RORAC of each asset in the portfolio (as defined in expression 6.3):

$$\text{RORAC}(\mathfrak{s}(\vec{u}^0)) =$$
$$\frac{u_1^0 \cdot r_1 + u_2^0 \cdot r_2}{-u_1^0 \cdot r_1 - u_2^0 \cdot r_2 + \Phi^{-1}(\alpha) \cdot \sqrt{(u_1^0)^2 + u_1^0 \cdot u_2^0 + (u_2^0)^2}},$$

$$\text{RORAC}(-u_1^0 \cdot Y_1 \mid \mathfrak{s}(\vec{u}^0))) =$$
$$\frac{u_1^0 \cdot r_1}{-u_1^0 \cdot r_1 + \Phi^{-1}(\alpha) \cdot \dfrac{(2 \cdot (u_1^0)^2 + u_1^0 \cdot u_2^0) \cdot \sqrt{(u_1^0)^2 + u_1^0 \cdot u_2^0 + (u_2^0)^2}}{2 \cdot ((u_1^0)^2 + u_1^0 \cdot u_2^0 + (u_2^0)^2)}}, \qquad (6.13)$$

$$\text{RORAC}(-u_2^0 \cdot Y_2 \mid \mathfrak{s}(\vec{u}^0))) =$$
$$\frac{u_2^0 \cdot r_2}{-u_2^0 \cdot r_2 + \Phi^{-1}(\alpha) \cdot \dfrac{(u_1^0 \cdot u_2^0 + 2 \cdot (u_2^0)^2) \cdot \sqrt{(u_1^0)^2 + u_1^0 \cdot u_2^0 + (u_2^0)^2}}{2 \cdot ((u_1^0)^2 + u_1^0 \cdot u_2^0 + (u_2^0)^2)}}.$$

Considering the aforementioned values of u_1^0, u_2^0, r_1, r_2, and α, the previous expressions lead to the following results:

$$\text{RORAC}(\mathfrak{s}(\vec{u}^0)) = \frac{1.5 \cdot 46.2098\% + 1.7 \cdot 46.3798\%}{-1.5 \cdot 46.2098\% - 1.7 \cdot 46.3798\% + 3.4316 \cdot 2.7731}$$
$$= 148.1605\%/803.4554\%$$
$$= 18.4404\%,$$

$$\text{RORAC}(-1.5 \cdot Y_1 \mid \mathfrak{s}(\vec{u}^0))) = \frac{1.5 \cdot 46.2098\%}{-1.5 \cdot 46.2098\% + 3.4316 \cdot \dfrac{7.05 \cdot 2.7731}{2 \cdot 7.69}}$$

$$= 69.3147\%/366.8941\%$$

$$= 18.8923\%,$$

$$\text{RORAC}(-1.7 \cdot Y_2 \mid \mathfrak{s}(\vec{u}^0))) = \frac{1.7 \cdot 46.3798\%}{-1.7 \cdot 46.3798\% + 3.4316 \cdot \dfrac{8.33 \cdot 2.7731}{2 \cdot 7.69}}$$

$$= 78.8457\%/436.5613\%$$

$$= 18.0606\%.$$

$$(6.14)$$

These results are providing us the following information: on the one hand, although it is expected that the current position on the second asset would generate a higher return (near 79%) than the current position on the first one (69%), the trade-off between risk and return measured by the portfolio-related RORAC is better for the position on the first asset than for the position on the second one. Additionally, the portfolio-related RORAC of the position on the first asset (18.8923%) is higher than the RORAC of the overall portfolio (18.4404%) which, in turn, is higher than the portfolio-related RORAC of the position on the second asset (18.0606%). As we know that within this allocation the RORAC compatibility is satisfied, a natural strategy to improve the RORAC of our current portfolio would be slightly increasing our position in the first asset and shorting our position in the second asset (also with a slight decrement of the position). For instance, it can be checked that if positions (u_1^0, u_2^0) are changed to be $(1.56, 1.69)$ instead of $(1.5, 1.7)$, then the RORAC of the overall portfolio becomes 18.4479% (an improvement is achieved).

This is a straight application of the RORAC compatibility property of RO-RAC contributions as stated in Definition 6.4. Note that this is not contradictory with the fact that an optimal portfolio (in terms of RORAC) would be found following a different strategy (for instance, increasing current positions in both assets at the same time). Why? Because the strategy of increasing both positions may be decomposed in several sub-strategies (steps) in which increasing or decreasing positions on the assets depend on the recalculated portfolio-related RORACs. Going back to the numerical example, after changing our portfolio to 1.56 units of the first asset and 1.69 units of the second one, it can be checked that $\text{RORAC}(-1.56 \cdot Y_1 \mid \mathfrak{s}(\vec{u}^0)) = 18.7133\%$ and $\text{RORAC}(-1.69 \cdot Y_2 \mid \mathfrak{s}(\vec{u}^0)) = 18.2104\%$. To improve the overall RORAC of the portfolio we could now decide to change again our positions, increasing to 1.69 our position on the first asset and freezing the position on the second one. By doing this, we would obtain an overall RORAC for our new portfolio equal to 18.4521% (higher than the 18.4479% obtained with the first change of positions). But now $\text{RORAC}(-1.69 \cdot Y_1 \mid \mathfrak{s}(\vec{u}^0)) = 18.4120\%$ and $\text{RORAC}(-1.69 \cdot Y_2 \mid \mathfrak{s}(\vec{u}^0)) = 18.4923\%$, which would drive us to make another change: we would increase our position on the second asset to, for example, 1.71 units and let the position on the first one equal to 1.69. If we do that then the RORAC of the overall portfolio slightly raises to 18.4522%. Is this portfolio with $(u_1^0, u_2^0) = (1.69, 1.71)$ optimal in terms of RORAC? We do not know, but its overall RORAC (18.4522%) is higher than the original one (18.4404%) and, as we have shown, original positions on both assets have increased.

This example has been adapted from Buch *et al.* [2011]. The interested reader can be found there examples showing the sub-optimality, in terms of the RORAC of the overall portfolio, of some strategies devised by properly applying the RORAC compatibility property that the contributions derived from the gradient allocation principle satisfy.

Some final comments on the gradient allocation principle. This elegant approach to proportional capital allocation principles based on partial contributions has two main drawbacks when they are applied on a real context. On the one hand, infinitesimal (or very small) perturbations on the risky position of an agent can often not be made in practice. Frequently, it is not feasible to perform arbitrarily small changes in positions. As a consequence, the compatibility of RORAC contributions should be barely satisfied even for the risk contributions linked to the gradient allocation principle.

The second limitation is related to the computation of risk contributions $(\partial f_{\vec{X}} / \partial u_i)(\vec{u})$, where the value of the risk measure ρ for sums $\mathfrak{s}(\vec{u})$, $\vec{u} \in \mathbb{R}^n$ cannot be expressed in an analytic closed-form expression. This is, probably, the most frequent practical situation. In most of the cases, some decisions must be taken in order to approximately do an allocation based on the gradient. For instance, Tasche [2007] shows how the risk contributions of X_i to the VaR_α of the portfolio can be approximated using kernel estimators. With this respect, it has to be noted that this situation is extremely similar to the one depicted in Figure 1.2 in Chapter 1, but now considering on the left hand side (Theory) a gradient allocation principle $\vec{K}$ and in the right hand side (Practice) the effective estimation of that capital allocation principle $\widehat{\vec{K}}$.

6.3.2   Other capital allocation principles based on partial contributions

There are other examples of proportional capital allocation principles based on partial contributions fitting expression (6.2). Two examples are given here, one from a probabilistic perspective and another one from a game-theoretic perspective.

The covariance allocation principle

This principle is proposed, for instance, in Overbeck [2000]. It takes into account the variance as the risk measure for the whole portfolio: $\rho(S) = \mathbb{V}(S)$. The partial contribution of the ith agent X_i is the covariance of X_i with respect to S, so $\rho(X_i \mid S) = \text{Cov}(X_i, S)$. Therefore, this principle is expressed as

$$K_i = K \cdot \frac{\text{Cov}(X_i, S)}{\mathbb{V}(S)}, \quad \forall i = 1, \ldots, n. \tag{6.15}$$

Note that $\rho(S) = \sum_{j=1}^{n} \rho(X_i \mid S)$ because of the (bi)linearity of the covariance:

$$\rho(S) = \mathbb{V}(S) = \text{Cov}(S, S) = \text{Cov}\left(\sum_{j=1}^{n} X_j, S\right) = \sum_{j=1}^{n} \text{Cov}(X_j, S) = \sum_{j=1}^{n} \rho(X_i \mid S).$$

From the perspective of the Euler's Theorem on homogeneous functions, this principle can be understood in two different (but related) ways. The first interpretation considers as the risk measure ρ the variance in expression (6.4), in order to interpret the covariance principle similarly to a gradient principle. The resulting function $f_{\vec{X}} = \mathbb{V} \circ \mathfrak{s}$ is not an homogeneous function of degree $r = 1$ but an *homogeneous function of degree $r = 2$*, because the variance is not a positively homogeneous risk measure but satisfies the following relationship: for all $\lambda \in \mathbb{R}$ and for all $X \in \Gamma$, $\mathbb{V}(\lambda \cdot X) = \lambda^2 \cdot \mathbb{V}(X)$. From Theorem 6.1 this means that expression

$$2 \cdot \mathbb{V}\left(\sum_{j=1}^{n} u_j \cdot X_j\right) = \sum_{i=1}^{n} u_i \cdot \frac{\partial \mathbb{V}\left(\sum_{k=1}^{n} u_k \cdot X_k\right)}{\partial u_i} \tag{6.16}$$

holds or, in other words, that

$$\left[\frac{1}{2} \cdot \frac{\partial \mathbb{V}\left(\sum_{k=1}^{n} u_k \cdot X_k\right)}{\partial u_i}\right]_{|\vec{u}=(1,1,\ldots,1)} = \text{Cov}(X_i, S).$$

Let us check this last equivalence:

$$
\begin{aligned}
\frac{\partial}{\partial u_i} \mathbb{V}\left(\sum_{j=1}^{n} u_j \cdot X_j \right) &= \frac{\partial}{\partial u_i} \mathrm{Cov}\left(\sum_{j=1}^{n} u_j \cdot X_j, \sum_{k=1}^{n} u_k \cdot X_k \right) \\
&= \frac{\partial}{\partial u_i} \left[\sum_{j=1}^{n} u_j \cdot \mathrm{Cov}\left(X_j, \sum_{k=1}^{n} u_k \cdot X_k \right) \right] \\
&= \frac{\partial}{\partial u_i} \left[\sum_{j=1}^{n} \sum_{k=1}^{n} u_j \cdot u_k \cdot \mathrm{Cov}(X_j, X_k) \right] \\
&= \frac{\partial}{\partial u_i} \left[\sum_{k=1}^{n} u_i \cdot u_k \cdot \mathrm{Cov}(X_i, X_k) \right. \\
&\qquad \left. + \sum_{j \neq i} \sum_{k=1}^{n} u_j \cdot u_k \cdot \mathrm{Cov}(X_j, X_k) \right] \\
&= \frac{\partial}{\partial u_i} \left[u_i^2 \cdot \mathrm{Cov}(X_i, X_i) + \sum_{k \neq i} u_i \cdot u_k \cdot \mathrm{Cov}(X_i, X_k) \right. \\
&\qquad + \sum_{j \neq i} \sum_{k \neq i} u_j \cdot u_k \cdot \mathrm{Cov}\left(X_j, X_k \right) \\
&\qquad \left. + \sum_{j \neq i} u_j \cdot u_i \cdot \mathrm{Cov}(X_j, X_i) \right] \\
&= 2 \cdot u_i \cdot \mathrm{Cov}(X_i, X_i) + 2 \cdot \sum_{k \neq i} u_k \cdot \mathrm{Cov}(X_i, X_k) \\
&= 2 \cdot \mathrm{Cov}(X_i, \mathfrak{s}(\vec{u}))
\end{aligned}
$$

If last expression is evaluated at $\vec{u} = (1, 1, \dots, 1)$ then the desired result is found.

The second interpretation allows to understand the covariance allocation principle as a pure gradient allocation principle as explained in Section 6.3.1. The key is to consider as the risk measure ρ in (6.4) the covariance of a random variable with respect to the sum S of the components of $\vec{X}$ instead of the variance. So the function $f_{\vec{X}}$ is taken as $f_{\vec{X}} = \mathrm{Cov}(\cdot, S) \circ \mathfrak{s}$. As long as $\mathrm{Cov}(\lambda \cdot X, S) = \lambda \cdot \mathrm{Cov}(X, S)$ for all $\lambda \in \mathbb{R}$ and for all $X \in \Gamma$, $f_{\vec{X}}$ is an homogeneous function of degree $r = 1$ and Theorem 6.1 may be applied in this case as in Proposition 6.1.

Example 6.3. Let us apply the covariance principle to obtain an allocation linked to the portfolio of Example 6.1.

The first step is to recall the expression for the variance of $(\mathfrak{s}(\vec{u}))$ and to derive the expression for the homogeneous (covariance) function:

$$\mathbb{V}(\mathfrak{s}(\vec{u})) = u_1^2 + u_1 \cdot u_2 + u_2^2,$$

$$\mathrm{Cov}(-u_1 \cdot Y_1, \mathfrak{s}(\vec{u})) = \mathbb{E}\left[(-u_1 \cdot Y_1 - \mathbb{E}(-u_1 \cdot Y_1)) \cdot (\mathfrak{s}(\vec{u}) - \mathbb{E}(\mathfrak{s}(\vec{u})))\right]$$
$$= \mathbb{E}\left[-u_1 \cdot X_1 \cdot \left(-u_1 \cdot X_1 - \frac{1}{2} \cdot u_2 \cdot X_1 - \frac{\sqrt{3}}{2} \cdot u_2 \cdot X_2\right)\right]$$
$$= u_1^2 + \frac{1}{2} \cdot u_1 \cdot u_2,$$

$$\mathrm{Cov}(-u_2 \cdot Y_2, \mathfrak{s}(\vec{u})) = \mathbb{E}\left[(-u_2 \cdot Y_2 - \mathbb{E}(-u_2 \cdot Y_2)) \cdot (\mathfrak{s}(\vec{u}) - \mathbb{E}(\mathfrak{s}(\vec{u})))\right]$$
$$= \mathbb{E}\left[\left(-\frac{1}{2} \cdot u_2 \cdot X_1 - \frac{\sqrt{3}}{2} \cdot u_2 \cdot X_2\right)\left(-u_1 \cdot X_1 - \frac{1}{2} \cdot u_2 \cdot X_1 - \frac{\sqrt{3}}{2} \cdot u_2 \cdot X_2\right)\right]$$
$$= \frac{1}{2} \cdot u_1 \cdot u_2 + u_2^2.$$

If $(u_1^0, u_2^0) = (1.5, 1.7)$ then $\mathbb{V}\left(\mathfrak{s}(\vec{u}^0)\right) = 7.69$, $\mathrm{Cov}\left(-1.5 \cdot Y_1, \mathfrak{s}(\vec{u}^0)\right) = 3.525$ and $\mathrm{Cov}\left(-1.7 \cdot Y_2, \mathfrak{s}(\vec{u}^0)\right) = 4.165$. In relative terms, the covariance allocation principle is assigning a 45.84% of the risk (measured by the variance) to the first asset and a 54.16% to the second one.

Finally, some comments on strengths and weaknesses of the covariance principle may be pointed out. As a strength in front of other gradient allocation principles, estimators of both $\mathbb{V}(S)$ and $\mathrm{Cov}(X_i, S)$ for all $i = 1, \ldots, n$ can be found satisfying that the sum of the estimated covariances add up to the estimated variance of the overall portfolio, whatever the set of random variables $\{X_i\}_{i=1,\ldots,n}$ is. Hence, the covariance principle overcomes the second drawback commented at the end of the previous section. As a weakness, the allocation only takes care of linear dependence structures between random variables X_i, $i = 1, \ldots, n$, and may lead to negative allocated capitals K_i. The article of Wang [2014] is inspired by the covariance allocation principle and the tail variance risk measure presented in Furman and Landsman [2006]. In this work the author define the capital allocation principles based on the Tail Covariance Premium Adjusted and tackles a possible non linear dependence between business lines.

The Shapley value principle and one of its simplifications

Another proportional allocation principle based on partial contributions can be derived from game theory. The capital allocation problem can be understood as a cooperative game in which capital K has to be *fairly* shared by the agents, taking into account that the cost of a coalition is linked to the risk that this coalition assumes. The key concept to find such a fair allocation is the Shapley value (sometimes also called Bondareva-Shapley value). Let us use the following notations: $N = \{1, \ldots, n\}$, $A \subseteq N$ denotes a subset of N with cardinality $a = |A|$ and $\mathcal{R}(A) = \rho\left(\sum_{k \in A} X_k\right)$. A capital allocation principle based on the Shapley value is of the form (6.2), where

$$\rho(X_i \mid S) = \sum_{A \subseteq N \smallsetminus \{i\}} \frac{a! \cdot (n - a - 1)!}{n!} \cdot [\mathcal{R}(A \cup \{i\}) - \mathcal{R}(A)] . \qquad (6.17)$$

Note that $\mathcal{R}(N) = \rho(S)$. Additionally, it can be proved that $\rho(S) = \sum_{i=1}^{n} \rho(X_i \mid S)$ using the properties of the Shapley value. The contribution of ith agent to the overall risk is, basically, a weighted average of all the marginal contributions that ith agent makes on the risk of each of the coalitions that can be obtained without ith agent. This principle can require a high computational demand for obtaining each $\rho(X_i \mid S)$ if n is large.

In order to avoid this drawback, some authors propose an alternative approach, that is a simplification of this principle. In Balog [2010] this alternative is called *incremental principle*. It is built by reducing the number of terms added up in expression (6.17) only to the one linked to the set $N \smallsetminus \{i\}$. In other words, the incremental principle is of the form (6.1) where

$$f_i(X_i) = \mathcal{R}(N) - \mathcal{R}(N \smallsetminus \{i\}) = \rho(S) - \rho\left(\sum_{j \neq i} X_j\right), \forall\, i = 1, \ldots, n.$$

This alternative principle assigns as partial contribution of ith agent the difference between the overall risk and the risk quantified in absence of the ith agent. To some extent, this principle can be considered as a hybrid between a proportional principle based on partial contributions and a stand-alone proportional principle. This principle cannot be considered a proportional principle based on partial contributions, because $\sum_{j=1}^{n} f_j(X_j) \neq \rho(S)$. But, at the same time, some relationship between ith agent and the rest of participants is taken into account by f_i, so it cannot be considered a stand-alone proportional principle. The loss of information is the price that must be paid to reduce the computational cost of the Shapley value for large n.

Example 6.4. Let us illustrate the Shapley value principle. We will consider three random variables, two of which are identical. They can only take four possible values. So, for the following states $(\omega_1, \omega_2, \omega_3, \omega_4)$, random variables

X_1, X_2 and X_3 are defined as follows:

$$X_1 \begin{pmatrix} \omega_1 \\ \omega_2 \\ \omega_3 \\ \omega_4 \end{pmatrix} = \begin{pmatrix} 60 \\ 30 \\ 0 \\ -15 \end{pmatrix}, \quad X_2 \begin{pmatrix} \omega_1 \\ \omega_2 \\ \omega_3 \\ \omega_4 \end{pmatrix} = X_3 \begin{pmatrix} \omega_1 \\ \omega_2 \\ \omega_3 \\ \omega_4 \end{pmatrix} = \begin{pmatrix} 3 \\ 30 \\ -7.5 \\ 15 \end{pmatrix}.$$

The corresponding probabilities are:

$$P \begin{pmatrix} \omega_1 \\ \omega_2 \\ \omega_3 \\ \omega_4 \end{pmatrix} = \begin{pmatrix} p_1 \\ p_2 \\ p_3 \\ p_4 \end{pmatrix} = \begin{pmatrix} 1/10 \\ 1/10 \\ 2/5 \\ 2/5 \end{pmatrix}.$$

This information can be displayed in a table, where $S = X_1 + X_2 + X_3$ and the other partial sums can also be computed.

Ω	P	X_1	X_2	X_3	$X_1 + X_{i=2,3}$	$X_2 + X_3$	S
ω_1	1/10	60	3	3	63	6	66
ω_2	1/10	0	30	30	30	60	60
ω_3	2/5	30	-7.5	-7.5	22.5	-15	15
ω_4	2/5	-15	15	15	0	30	15

The reader can easily compute the survival function for each of the random variables. Let us show how to compute the probability distribution function and the survival function for S, namely the sum of the three initial random variables.

Ω	P	S	F_S	S_S
ω_3	2/5	15	4/5	1/5
ω_4	2/5	15	4/5	1/5
ω_2	1/10	60	9/10	1/10
ω_1	1/10	66	1	0

The question is now to illustrate how to perform the allocation of a risk measure based on the Shapley principle. Let us consider the $\text{TVaR}_{85\%}(S)$. Then, the following measures are needed: $\text{TVaR}_{85\%}(X_1)$, $\text{TVaR}_{85\%}(X_2)$, $\text{TVaR}_{85\%}(X_3)$, $\text{TVaR}_{85\%}(X_1 + X_{i=2,3})$, $\text{TVaR}_{85\%}(X_2 + X_3)$ and, obviously, $\text{TVaR}_{85\%}(S)$.

Recall (see, Chapter 1, eq. (1.4)) that an expression for the $\text{TVaR}_\alpha(Z)$, for a random variable Z, is:

$$\text{TVaR}_\alpha(Z) = \text{VaR}_\alpha(Z) + \frac{1}{1-\alpha} \cdot \text{ES}_\alpha(Z). \qquad (6.18)$$

Then since, $\text{VaR}_{85\%}(S) = 60$ and

$$\text{ES}_{85\%}(S) = \sum_{j=1}^{4}(s_j - \text{VaR}_{85\%}(S))_+ \cdot p_j = (66-60) \cdot \frac{1}{10} = \frac{6}{10}, \qquad (6.19)$$

it follows that

$$\text{TVaR}_{85\%}(S) = 60 + \frac{100}{15} \cdot \frac{6}{10} = 60 + \frac{60}{15} = 64. \qquad (6.20)$$

Similarly, $\text{TVaR}_{85\%}(X_1) = 50$ and $\text{TVaR}_{85\%}(X_2) = \text{TVaR}_{85\%}(X_3) = 25$, while $\text{TVaR}_{85\%}(X_1 + X_{i=2,3}) = 52$ and $\text{TVaR}_{85\%}(X_2 + X_3) = 50$.
Since all the necessary values of the risk measure $\rho = \text{TVaR}_{85\%}$ are ready, then two tables are constructed in order to obtain $\rho(X_1 \mid S)$, $\rho(X_2 \mid S)$ and $\rho(X_3 \mid S)$. Let us first concentrate on X_1.

A	$\sum_{k \in A} X_k$	a	$a!$	$\frac{(n-a-1)!}{n!}$	$X_1 + \sum_{k \in A} X_k$	$\mathscr{R}(A)$	$\mathscr{R}(A \cup \{1\})$
$\varnothing$	$\varnothing$	0	1	2/6	X_1	0	50
$\{2\}$	X_2	1	1	1/6	$X_1 + X_2$	25	52
$\{3\}$	X_3	1	1	1/6	$X_1 + X_3$	25	52
$\{2,3\}$	$X_2 + X_3$	2	2	1/6	S	50	64

Using expression (6.17), it follows that:

$$\rho(X_1 \mid S) = \frac{2}{6} \cdot (50-0) + \frac{1}{6} \cdot (52-25) + \frac{1}{6} \cdot (52-25) + \frac{2}{6} \cdot (64-50)$$
$$= 30 + \frac{1}{3}$$

Using a similar procedure, it follows that $\rho(X_2 \mid S) = \rho(X_3 \mid S) = 16 + 5/6$. Therefore, $\rho(S) = \sum_{i=1}^{3} \rho(X_i \mid S) = 64$.

6.3.3   The excess based allocation principle

The last principle explained in this chapter is the principle proposed in van Gulick *et al.* [2012]. The reason is twofold. On the one hand, because of its originality and, on the other hand, because of its non-proportionality. Taken the authors' own words [cf. page 29].

"The allocation rule that we propose determines the allocation that lexicographically minimizes the portfolio's excesses among a set of allocations that satisfies two basic properties. First, no portfolio is allocated more risk capital than the amount of risk capital that it would need to withhold if it were on its own. Second, a portfolio is not allocated less than the minimum loss it can incur".

To better understand this principle, the following definition from van Gulick *et al.* [2012] must be presented.

Definition 6.5 (Lexicographical ordering). For $m \in \mathbb{N}$ and any two vectors $\vec{x}, \vec{y} \in \mathbb{R}^n$, $\vec{x}$ is lexicographically strictly smaller than $\vec{y}$, denoted as $\vec{x} <_{\text{lex}} \vec{y}$, if there exists an $i \leq m$ such that $x_i < y_i$, and for all $j < i$ it holds that $x_j = y_j$. Moreover, $\vec{x}$ is lexicographically smaller than $\vec{y}$, denoted by $\vec{x} \leq_{\text{lex}} \vec{y}$, if $\vec{x} = \vec{y}$ or $\vec{x} <_{\text{lex}} \vec{y}$.

The authors considers that the capital K to be shared among the agents is, in fact, equal to $\rho(S)$, where ρ should be a coherent risk measure. They use notation $N = \{1, \dots, n\}$. Once these preliminaries are established, the idea of the excess based allocation principle may be outlined in four steps:

(i) Consider any capital allocation principle $\vec{K}$ such that $\sum_{j=1}^n K_j = \rho(S)$ and such that the following boundary conditions are satisfied for all $i \in N$: $\max\{0, \min_{\omega \in \Omega} X_i(\omega)\} \leq K_i \leq \rho(X_i)$. The set of all the principles satisfying these conditions is called the *set of feasible principles*, denoted as $\mathfrak{F}$.

(ii) Compute, for each feasible principle, the vector of dimension 2^n consisting in $\bar{e}(\vec{K}) = \left(\mathbb{E}\left[\left(\sum_{j \in A} (X_j - K_j) \right)_+ \right] \right)_{A \subseteq N}$. So, there is a component for each subset $A \subseteq N$. This component is equal to the mathematical expectation of the random variable that represents the non-negative excess of capital that principle $\vec{K}$ assigns to coalition A.

(iii) For each feasible principle $\vec{K}$, the components of $\bar{e}(\vec{K})$ are ordered in a decreasing manner. The ordered resulting vector in $\mathbb{R}^n$ is denoted by $\theta[\bar{e}(\vec{K})]$.

(iv) The excess based allocation principle, denoted by $\vec{K}_{EBA}$, is the feasible principle which lexicographically minimizes the $\theta[\bar{e}(\vec{K})]$. In other words, $\vec{K}_{EBA}$ is chosen among all feasible principles as the principle associated to the first position in the set of ordered $\theta[\bar{e}(\vec{K})]$, supposing that this order is similar to the one provided by a librarian who has been increasingly ordering vectors $\theta[\bar{e}(\vec{K})]$ alphabetically.

Obviously, last comment on step (iv) is not formal. A more precise way to present the excess based allocation principle is by

$$\vec{K}_{EBA} = \{\vec{K} \in \mathfrak{F} \mid \quad \theta[\bar{e}(\vec{K})] \leqslant_{\text{lex}} \theta[\bar{e}(\vec{C})], \quad \forall \vec{C} \in \mathfrak{F}\}, \tag{6.21}$$

taking into account that the set at the right-hand side of expression (6.21) is a single value set [as proved in van Gulick *et al.*, 2012] and that, therefore, there is a simplification of notation when identifying a set consisting on a single element with that element.

Although this perspective on the allocation procedure is very interesting, as in the case of the capital allocation principle based on the Shapley value, this principle can involve a significant computational cost when n is large. In addition, as long as the coherence property is required to the risk measure ρ to be used in the EBA principle, it has to be noted that VaR could not be used as ρ in that allocation procedure.

Example 6.5. The same random variables that were defined in the previous example (6.4) are used here to illustrate the excess based allocation principle, using $\text{TVaR}_{85\%}$.
The following steps are needed:

a) Conditions to be fulfilled by each feasible principle.

b) Calculation of vectors $\bar{e}(\vec{K})$.

c) Ordering the components of $\bar{e}(\vec{K})$, to obtain $\theta[\bar{e}(\vec{K})]$.

d) Finding the excess based allocation.

a) A feasible principle $\vec{K} = (K_1, K_2, K_3)$ has to fulfill the following conditions:

Condition 1. $K = K_1 + K_2 + K_3$. Since $K = \text{TVaR}_{85\%}(S) = 64$, then $K_1 + K_2 + K_3 = 64$.

Condition 2. $K_2 = K_3$, because the excess based allocation principle satisfies the symmetry property.

Condition 3. Condition $\max\{0, \min_{\omega \in \Omega} X_i(\omega)\} \leqslant K_i \leqslant \rho(X_i)$ in this case correspond to $0 \leqslant K_1 \leqslant 50$ and $0 \leqslant K_2 \leqslant 25$ (similarly, $0 \leqslant K_3 \leqslant 25$). Since by Condition 1 $K_2 = K_3 = (64 - K_1)/2$ it follows that $(64 - K_1)/2 = K_2 \leqslant 25$ then $14 \leqslant K_1$.

Moreover, no sub-portfolio should be allocated more capital than its own risk. Therefore, $K_1 + K_2 \leqslant \rho(K_1 + K_2) = 52$ and then, since $K_2 = (64 - K_1)/2$, it follows that $K_1 + (64 - K_1)/2 \leqslant \rho(K_1 + K_2) = 52$ and so, $K_1 \leqslant 40$. Then, the final conditions are:

$$14 \leqslant K_1 \leqslant 40$$

$$K_2 = K_3 = \frac{64 - K_1}{2}.$$

b) Vector $\bar{e}(\vec{K})$ has eight components, corresponding respectively to $\varnothing$, $\{1\}$, $\{2\}$, $\{3\}$, $\{1, 2\}$, $\{1, 3\}$, $\{2, 3\}$ and $\{1, 2, 3\}$. It can be written as follows:

$$\bar{e}(\vec{K}) = \begin{pmatrix} 0 \\ \begin{cases} (60 - K_1)/10 & \text{if } K_1 < 30 \\ (36 - K_1)/2 & \text{if } K_1 \leqslant 30 \end{cases} \\ \begin{cases} (K_1 - 4)/20 & \text{if } K_1 < 34 \\ (K_1 - 28)/4 & \text{if } K_1 \leqslant 34 \end{cases} \\ \begin{cases} (K_1 - 4)/20 & \text{if } K_1 < 34 \\ (K_1 - 28)/4 & \text{if } K_1 \leqslant 34 \end{cases} \\ (62 - K_1)/20 \\ (62 - K_1)/20 \\ \begin{cases} (K_1 - 4)/10 & \text{if } K_1 < 34 \\ (K_1 - 28)/4 & \text{if } K_1 \leqslant 34 \end{cases} \\ 1/5 \end{pmatrix}.$$

Note that the vector can be parametrized in terms of K_1.

c) Ordering depends on the values of K_1. Therefore, for instance if $K_1 = 14$, then the decreasing order is, in terms of the subsets of N, $\{1\} > \{1, 2\} = \{1, 3\} > \{2, 3\} > \{2\} = \{3\} > N > \varnothing$.

The ordering is different for each of the following intervals of K_1, namely $[14, 23 + 1/3]$, $[23 + 1/3, 32]$, $[32, 33]$, $[33, 260/7]$ and $[260/7, 40]$. Due to linearity, we only need to concentrate on the extremes of the previous intervals in order to find the candidates for the excess based allocation principle.

d) To finalize the computation of the allocation principle, we need to choose the principle that minimizes lexicographically the $\theta[\bar{e}(\vec{K})]$. We will first choose the principle in each interval and then find the overall choice. So,

In the interval $K_1 \in [14, 23 + 1/3]$, the minimum is found for $\{1\}$ and it is given by $K_1 = 23+1/3$, so $\vec{K}_{[14,23+1/3]} = (23+1/3, 20+1/3, 20+1/3)$, because $K_2 = (64 - K_1)/2$. Moreover, $\bar{e}(\vec{K}_{[14,23+1/3]}) = (6.\dot{3}, 1.9\dot{3}, 1.9\dot{3}, 1.9\dot{3}, 0.9\dot{6}, 0.9\dot{6}, 0.2, 0)$.

In the interval $K_1 \in [23 + 1/3, 32]$, the minimum is at $\{1\}$ and it is given by $K_1 = 32$, so $\vec{K}_{[23+1/3,32]} = (32, 16, 16)$. Here $\bar{e}(\vec{K}_{[23+1/3,32]}) = (2.8, 2.8, 1.5, 1.5, 1.4, 1.4, 0.2, 0)$, corresponding respectively to $\{1\} > \{2, 3\} > \{1, 2\} = \{1, 3\} > \{2\} = \{3\} > N > \varnothing$.

In the interval $K_1 \in [32, 33]$, the minimum is now at $\{2, 3\}$ and it is given by $K_1 = 32$, so again $\vec{K}_{[32,33]} = (32, 16, 16)$ and $\bar{e}(\vec{K}_{[32,33]}) = (2.8, 2.8, 1.5, 1.5, 1.4, 1.4, 0.2, 0)$, corresponding respectively to $\{2, 3\} > \{1\} > \{1, 2\} = \{1, 3\} > \{2\} = \{3\} > N > \varnothing$.

In the interval $K_1 \in [33, 260/7]$, the minimum is at $\{2, 3\}$ and it is given by $K_1 = 33$, so again $\vec{K}_{[33,260/7]} = (33, 15.5, 15.5)$ and $\bar{e}(\vec{K}_{[33,260/7]}) = (2.9, 2.7, 1.45, 1.45, 1.45, 1.45, 0.2, 0)$, corresponding respectively to $\{2, 3\} > \{1\} > \{2\} = \{3\} > \{1, 2\} = \{1, 3\} > N > \varnothing$.

In the interval $K_1 \in [260/7, 40]$, the minimum is at $\{2, 3\}$ and it is given by $K_1 = 260/6$, so again $\vec{K}_{[260/7,40]} = (37.14, 13.43, 13.43)$ and $\bar{e}(\vec{K}_{[260/7,40]}) = (4.57, 2.286, 2.286, 2.286, 1.2426, 1.2426, 0.2, 0)$, corresponding respectively to $\{2, 3\} > \{2\} = \{3\} > \{1\} > \{1, 2\} = \{1, 3\} > N > \varnothing$.

In the previous allocations, we seek the lexicographical minimum, which corresponds to $\bar{e}(\vec{K}_{[23+1/3,32]}) = \bar{e}(\vec{K}_{[32,33]}) = (2.8, 2.8, 1.5, 1.5, 1.4, 1.4, 0.2, 0)$. As a result, the excess based allocation principle is:

$$\vec{K} = (K_1, K_2, K_3) = (32, 16, 16).$$

Note that in van Gulick *et al.* [2012], the authors recommend an optimization procedure, which has not been implemented in the previous example.

6.4   Further reading

There is a large number of academic works related to capital allocation problems. An extensive literature can be found discussing solutions to capital allocation problems [see, among others. Denault, 2001; Kalkbrener, 2005; Tsanakas, 2009; Buch *et al.*, 2011; van Gulick *et al.*, 2012]. A number of recent studies focus on specific probability distributions of losses [Cossette *et al.*, 2012, 2013], risk dependence structures [Cai and Wei, 2014], asymptotics of capital allocations based on commonly used risk measures [Asimit *et al.*, 2011] or modifications of the optimization function to overcome limitations of allocations based on minimizing the loss function [Xu and Hu, 2012; Xu and Mao, 2013]. More precisely, You and Li [2014] analyze capital allocation problems concerning mutually interdependent risks, mainly where they are tied through an Archimedean copula. Wang [2014] investigates the usefulness of the Tail Covariance Premium Adjusted principle in the case of two business lines with exponentially distributed losses, where their dependence structure corresponds to a Farlie-Gumbel-Morgenstern copula. Zaks and Tsanakas [2014] generalize the framework proposed in Dhaene *et al.* [2012b], allowing the inclusion of different hierarchical levels of preferences about risk in the final solution. In Urbina and Guillen [2014] several principles are examined to solve a capital allocation problem related to operational risk. This list of academic contributions on capital allocation problems is not exhaustive. In fact, this topic is object of ongoing research. Two recent contributions are Tsanakas and Millossovich [2016] and Li and You [2015].

6.5   Exercices

1. Compare the allocation in percentage to each risk, obtained in the examples corresponding to the Shapley allocation principle and the excess based allocation principle.

2. Compute the RORAC for the risks described in Example 6.5.

3. Compute the gradient allocation principle which was illustrated in Example 6.1, but now using a different level $\alpha = 95\%$. You should discuss the consequences on that principle of diminishing the confidence level.

4. Consider again Example 6.1 and change the risk measure to another one, for instance TVaR. Compare the results with the ones obtained for the VaR.

7 Capital allocation based on GlueVaR

In Section 6.1 of the previous chapter a set of elements to fully describe a capital allocation problem were identified. Nonetheless, two of those elements are of main importance: the assignment criterion and the functions used to simplify the information provided by each random loss. So, one could think that guidelines about how capital should be shared among firm's units are basically defined in terms of two components: (1) a capital allocation criterion and (2) a risk measure. The choice of the specific form for each component is essential as different capital allocation solutions result from the specific selected combinations.

In this chapter we consider the framework suggested by Dhaene *et al.* [2012b]. Under this framework, capital allocation principles are interpreted as solutions to optimization problems. This approach has been followed in the recent literature [see, for instance You and Li, 2014; Zaks and Tsanakas, 2014].

7.1 A capital allocation framework

Most of the proportional allocation principles can be described in the framework suggested by Dhaene *et al.* [2012b]. Under this unifying framework a capital allocation problem is represented by means of three elements: a non-negative function (which is usually linked to a norm), a set of weights, and a set of auxiliary random variables. However, the Haircut allocation principle could not be fitted into this framework despite its simplicity: the Haircut allocation principle combines a stand-alone proportional capital allocation criterion with the classical Value at Risk.

Here, the extension of the framework due to Dhaene *et al.* [2012b] is described. This was suggested in Belles-Sampera *et al.* [2014b]. A slight modification of the original framework was proposed, consisting in relaxing some of the conditions in order to allow the inclusion of the Haircut capital allocation principle.

Assume that a capital $K > 0$ has to be allocated across n business units denoted by $i = 1, \ldots, n$. Any capital allocation problem can be described as the optimization problem given by

$$\min_{K_1, K_2, \ldots, K_n} \sum_{j=1}^{n} v_j \cdot \mathbb{E}\left[\zeta_j \cdot D\left(\frac{X_j - K_j}{v_j}\right)\right] \quad \text{s.t.} \quad \sum_{j=1}^{n} K_j = K, \qquad (7.1)$$

with the following characterizing elements:

(a) a function $D : \mathbb{R} \to \mathbb{R}^+$;

(b) a set of positive weights v_i, $i = 1, \ldots, n$, such that $\sum_{i=1}^{n} v_i = 1$; and

(c) a set of random variables ζ_i, $i = 1, \ldots, n$, with $\mathbb{E}[\zeta_i] < +\infty$.

Unlike the original framework provided by Dhaene *et al.* [2012b], a distinction is made in (c) so that each ζ_i is now no longer forced to be positive with each $\mathbb{E}[\zeta_i]$ equal to 1.

To conclude, there exist a relationship between this capital allocation framework and aggregation functions. Aggregation functions may be defined as solutions to optimization problems, as proposed in De Baets [2013]. Capital allocation problems are disaggregation problems and therefore, to some extent, the goal of capital allocation principles is the opposite of the goal of aggregation functions, which is a summarizing purpose. Nonetheless, the optimization perspective taken into account in expression (7.1) involves aggregation operators in the objective function. For instance, one can think of the function $\mathbb{E}\left[\sum_{j=1}^{n} v_j \cdot \zeta_j \cdot D\left(\frac{X_j - K_j}{v_j}\right)\right]$ to be minimized in (7.1) as the composition of two main aggregation operators: one aggregation operator is given by expression $\sum_{j=1}^{n} v_j \cdot \zeta_j \cdot D\left(\frac{X_j - K_j}{v_j}\right)$ and the other one is the mathematical expectation $\mathbb{E}$. It has to be noted that a similar perspective is proposed in Xu and Hu [2012], where the first aggregation function may be represented as $\Psi(L(\vec{K})) = \Psi\left(\sum_{j=1}^{n} \psi(X_j - K_j)\right)$, where ψ is a function usually linked to a distance and Ψ an increasing function (which could be the identity function, for instance).

7.2   The Haircut capital allocation principle

Following the modification that we proposed in Belles-Sampera *et al.* [2014b], the Haircut capital allocation solution can be obtained from the minimization problem (7.1). If a capital $K > 0$ has to be allocated across n business units, the Haircut allocation principle states that the capital K_i to be assigned to each business unit must be

$$K_i = K \cdot \frac{F_{X_i}^{-1}(\alpha)}{\sum\limits_{j=1}^{n} F_{X_j}^{-1}(\alpha)}, \quad \forall\, i = 1,\dots,n, \qquad (7.2)$$

where X_i is the random loss linked to the ith business unit, $F_{X_i}^{-1}$ is the inverse of the cumulative distribution function of X_i and $\alpha \in (0,1)$ is a given confidence level.

Let us consider $d_i = \min\{d \geq 1 \mid 0 < |M^d[X_i]| < +\infty\}$ for all $i = 1,\dots,n$, where $M^d[X_i] = \mathbb{E}[X_i^d]$ is the moment of order $d > 0$ of random variable X_i. Note that $d_i \geq 1$ for each i to face a feasible capital allocation problem. In other words, if a business unit presents a random loss with no finite moments, then the risk taken by that business unit is not insurable/hedgeable. The approach for fitting the Haircut allocation principle in the framework linked to the optimization problem (7.1) can be summarized as follows: if a constant r_i must be expressed as $r_i = \mathbb{E}[\zeta_i \cdot X_i]$, then using $\zeta_i = \frac{X_i^{d_i-1}}{M^{d_i}[X_i]} \cdot r_i$, a solution is found because $\mathbb{E}[\zeta_i \cdot X_i] = \mathbb{E}[(X_i^{d_i}/M^{d_i}[X_i])] \cdot r_i = r_i$. Although this is an elegant approach, the interpretation of the transformation made by ζ_i on X_i is intricate.

Proposition 7.1. *Let us consider a confidence level $\alpha \in (0,1)$. Then, the three characterizing elements required to represent the Haircut allocation principle in the general framework defined by (7.1) are:*

(a) $D(x) = x^2$,

(b) $v_i = \dfrac{\mathbb{E}[\zeta_i \cdot X_i]}{\sum\limits_{j=1}^{n} \mathbb{E}[\zeta_j \cdot X_j]}$, $i = 1,\dots,n$; *and*

(c) $\zeta_i = \dfrac{X_i^{d_i-1}}{M^{d_i}[X_i]} \cdot F_{X_i}^{-1}(\alpha)$, $i = 1,\dots,n$.

Proof. In this setting, it is straightforward to show that the solution $\vec{K} = (K_1, K_2, \ldots, K_n)$ to the minimization problem (7.1) is the Haircut allocation solution expressed by (7.2). Dhaene *et al.* [2012b] show that, if function D is the squared Euclidean norm $(D(x) = x^2)$, then any solution to (7.1) can be written as

$$K_i = \mathbb{E}[\zeta_i \cdot X_i] + v_i \cdot \left(K - \sum_{j=1}^n \mathbb{E}[\zeta_j \cdot X_j] \right), \quad \text{for all } i = 1, \ldots, n. \quad (7.3)$$

In this setting, $v_i = \mathbb{E}[\zeta_i \cdot X_i] / \sum_{j=1}^n \mathbb{E}[\zeta_j \cdot X_j]$ for each i, so

$$K_i = \mathbb{E}[\zeta_i \cdot X_i] + K \cdot \frac{\mathbb{E}[\zeta_i \cdot X_i]}{\sum\limits_{j=1}^n \mathbb{E}[\zeta_j \cdot X_j]} - \mathbb{E}[\zeta_i \cdot X_i] = K \cdot \frac{\mathbb{E}[\zeta_i \cdot X_i]}{\sum\limits_{j=1}^n \mathbb{E}[\zeta_j \cdot X_j]}.$$

And, finally, for all i it holds that $\mathbb{E}[\zeta_i \cdot X_i] = F_{X_i}^{-1}(\alpha)$ because of (c). Therefore, each K_i in the solution $\vec{K}$ is given by

$$K_i = K \cdot \frac{F_{X_i}^{-1}(\alpha)}{\sum\limits_{j=1}^n F_{X_j}^{-1}(\alpha)}.$$

$\square$

Some comments on v_i weights and ζ_i auxiliary random variables follow. Capital allocation principles driven by (7.3) can be thought of as two step allocation procedures: in a first step, a particular quantity $(C_i = \mathbb{E}[\zeta_i \cdot X_i])$ is allocated to each business unit. As the sum of all these quantities does not necessarily equal K (i.e., $\sum_{j=1}^n C_j \neq K$), in the second step the difference $\left(K - \sum_{j=1}^n C_j \right)$ is allocated to the business units considering weights v_i. From this perspective, C_i capitals are expected values of X_i losses restricted to particular events of interest and, therefore, ζ_i auxiliary random variables are used to select those events of interest for each business unit. On the other hand, v_i weights are related to the second step of the procedure, indicating how the difference between K and $\sum_{j=1}^n C_j$ must be distributed among business units. For a deeper interpretation of v_i weights and ζ_i auxiliary random variables in more general cases, the interested reader is referred to Dhaene *et al.* [2012b].

A remark on the gradient allocation principle. This principle can be fitted into the framework introduced by Dhaene *et al.* [2012b] following a similar strategy than the one in Proposition 7.1, but changing $F_{X_i}^{-1}(\alpha)$ by $\dfrac{\partial \rho}{\partial u_i}(S)$ for all $i = 1, \ldots, n$. Or, in other words,

$$D(x) = x^2, \quad v_i = \frac{\mathbb{E}[\zeta_i \cdot X_i]}{\displaystyle\sum_{j=1}^{n} \mathbb{E}[\zeta_j \cdot X_j]} \quad \text{and} \quad \zeta_i = \left(\frac{X_i^{d_i - 1}}{M^{d_i}[X_i]} \right) \cdot \frac{\partial \rho}{\partial u_i}(S)$$

for all $i = 1, \ldots, n$. Therefore, we find again that the gradient allocation principle is a proportional principle based on partial contributions, although we have now used a side track to arrive to this conclusion.

7.3 Proportional risk capital allocation principles using GlueVaR

The three characteristic elements of the framework suggested by Dhaene *et al.* [2012b] are function D, weights v_i and a set of appropriate ζ_i, for all $i = 1, \ldots, n$. According to the notation used by Dhaene *et al.* [2012b], we deal with business unit driven proportional allocation principles when ζ_i depends on X_i. If ζ_i depends on $S = \sum_{i=1}^{n} X_i$ then we have aggregate portfolio driven proportional allocation principles. In the former case, the marginal risk contributions of business units to the overall risk of the portfolio are not taken into account; in the latter, they are. Adopting the notation introduced in the previous chapter, principles belonging to the first category are here denoted as stand-alone proportional allocation principles while principles in the second category are denoted as proportional allocation principles based on partial contributions.

In this chapter, two GlueVaR based proportional capital allocation principles that we suggested in Belles-Sampera *et al.* [2014b] are presented. Both principles share the expressions for two of the three characterizing elements:

$$D(x) = x^2 \text{ and } v_i = \frac{\mathbb{E}[\zeta_i \cdot X_i]}{\displaystyle\sum_{j=1}^{n} \mathbb{E}[\zeta_j \cdot X_j]}, \text{ for all } i = 1, \ldots, n.$$

They differ in the set of random variables ζ_i, $i = 1, \ldots, n$, which are presented below for the case of continuous random variables X_i.

7.3.1   Stand-alone proportional allocation principles using GlueVaR

Given two confidence levels α and β in $(0,1)$, $\alpha < \beta$, and two distorted survival probabilities h_1 and h_2, if ζ_i is fixed as

$$\zeta_i = \omega_1 \cdot \frac{\mathbb{1}\left[X_i \geq F_{X_i}^{-1}(\beta)\right]}{1-\beta} + \omega_2 \cdot \frac{\mathbb{1}\left[X_i \geq F_{X_i}^{-1}(\alpha)\right]}{1-\alpha}$$
$$+ \omega_3 \cdot \frac{X_i^{d_i-1}}{M^{d_i}[X_i]} \cdot F_{X_i}^{-1}(\alpha), \quad \text{for all } i = 1,\dots,n, \qquad (7.4)$$

then the stand-alone proportional allocation principle using as risk measure the $\text{GlueVaR}_{\beta,\alpha}^{h_1,h_2}$ can be represented in the modified capital allocation framework explained in Section 7.1. Components of the solution $(K_1, K_2, \dots, K_n)$ are expressed as

$$K_i = K \cdot \frac{\text{GlueVaR}_{\beta,\alpha}^{h_1,h_2}(X_i)}{\sum_{j=1}^{n} \text{GlueVaR}_{\beta,\alpha}^{h_1,h_2}(X_j)}, \quad \text{for all } i = 1,\dots,n. \qquad (7.5)$$

7.3.2   Proportional allocation principles based on partial contributions using GlueVaR

Similarly, if there exists a confidence level $\alpha^* \in (0,1)$ such that $F_S^{-1}(\alpha) = \sum_{j=1}^{n} F_{X_j}^{-1}(\alpha^*)$, the proportional allocation principle based on partial contributions using $\text{GlueVaR}_{\beta,\alpha}^{h_1,h_2}$ can be fitted to the modified capital allocation framework detailed in Section 7.1. In this case, ζ_i has to be equal to

$$\zeta_i = \omega_1 \cdot \frac{\mathbb{1}\left[S \geq F_S^{-1}(\beta)\right]}{1-\beta} + \omega_2 \cdot \frac{\mathbb{1}\left[S \geq F_S^{-1}(\alpha)\right]}{1-\alpha}$$
$$+ \omega_3 \cdot \frac{X_i^{d_i-1}}{M^{d_i}[X_i]} \cdot F_{X_i}^{-1}(\alpha^*), \quad \text{for all } i = 1,\dots,n. \qquad (7.6)$$

Each component of the solution $(K_1, K_2, \dots, K_n)$ is then obtained as

$$K_i = K \cdot \left[\omega_1 \cdot \frac{\mathbb{E}\left[X_i \mid S \geq F_S^{-1}(\beta)\right]}{\text{GlueVaR}_{\beta,\alpha}^{h_1,h_2}(S)} + \omega_2 \cdot \frac{\mathbb{E}\left[X_i \mid S \geq F_S^{-1}(\alpha)\right]}{\text{GlueVaR}_{\beta,\alpha}^{h_1,h_2}(S)} \right.$$
$$\left. + \omega_3 \cdot \frac{F_{X_i}^{-1}(\alpha^*)}{\text{GlueVaR}_{\beta,\alpha}^{h_1,h_2}(S)} \right]. \qquad (7.7)$$

Alternatively, another approach can be considered. There exists a set of confidence levels $\alpha_j \in (0,1)$, for all $j = 1, \ldots, n$, such that $F_S^{-1}(\alpha) = \sum_{j=1}^n F_{X_j}^{-1}(\alpha_j)$. Therefore, the proportional allocation principle based on partial contributions using $\text{GlueVaR}_{\beta,\alpha}^{h_1,h_2}$ can also be fitted to the modified capital allocation framework. In this case, ζ_i have to be equal to

$$\zeta_i = \omega_1 \cdot \frac{\mathbb{1}\left[S \geqslant F_S^{-1}(\beta)\right]}{1-\beta} + \omega_2 \cdot \frac{\mathbb{1}\left[S \geqslant F_S^{-1}(\alpha)\right]}{1-\alpha}$$

$$+ \omega_3 \cdot \frac{X_i^{d_i-1}}{M^{d_i}[X_i]} \cdot F_{X_i}^{-1}(\alpha_i), \quad \text{for all } i = 1, \ldots, n. \qquad (7.8)$$

Each component of the solution $(K_1, K_2, \ldots, K_n)$ is then obtained as

$$K_i = K \cdot \left[\omega_1 \cdot \frac{\mathbb{E}\left[X_i \mid S \geqslant F_S^{-1}(\beta)\right]}{\text{GlueVaR}_{\beta,\alpha}^{h_1,h_2}(S)} + \omega_2 \cdot \frac{\mathbb{E}\left[X_i \mid S \geqslant F_S^{-1}(\alpha)\right]}{\text{GlueVaR}_{\beta,\alpha}^{h_1,h_2}(S)} \right.$$

$$\left. + \omega_3 \cdot \frac{F_{X_i}^{-1}(\alpha_i)}{\text{GlueVaR}_{\beta,\alpha}^{h_1,h_2}(S)} \right]. \qquad (7.9)$$

A final comment related to non-proportional capital allocation principles using GlueVaR. It has to be mentioned that it is possible and straightforward to obtain non-proportional principles using any of the auxiliary random variables ζ_i described in expressions (7.4), (7.6) or (7.8). If function $D(x) = x^2$, then the only thing that must be taken into account is that at least one of the weights v_i, $i = 1, \ldots, n$, must be different from $\mathbb{E}[\zeta_i \cdot X_i]/\left(\sum_{j=1}^n \mathbb{E}[\zeta_j \cdot X_j]\right)$. Under these restrictions, whatever set of auxiliary random variables $\vec{\zeta}$ is chosen among expressions (7.4), (7.6) or (7.8), non-proportional capital allocation principles $\vec{K}$ using GlueVaR are obtained through expression (7.3).

7.4   An example of insurance risk capital allocation using GlueVaR on claim costs

Data of previous chapters are used to illustrate the application of capital allocation principles based on GlueVaR risk measures. Table 7.1 shows risk values for this example. The last column presents diversification benefit, which is the difference between the sum of the risks of X_1, X_2 and X_3 and the risk of $X_1 + X_2 + X_3$. In this example, VaR$_{95\%}$ and one of the GlueVaR risk measures are not subadditive in the whole domain.

Table 7.1   Risk assessment of claim costs using GlueVaR risk measures

	X_1	X_2	X_3	$X_1 + X_2 + X_3$	Difference[*]
	(a)	(b)	(c)	(d)	(a)+(b)+(d)-(c)
$VaR_{95\%}$	2.5	0.6	1.1	5.9	−1.7
$TVaR_{95\%}$	12.5	8.0	1.3	19.7	2.1
$TVaR_{99.5\%}$	40.8	42.1	1.8	81.1	3.6
$GlueVaR_{99.5\%,95\%}^{11/30,2/3}$	18.6	16.9	1.4	35.6	1.3
$GlueVaR_{99.5\%,95\%}^{0,1}$	9.4	4.2	1.2	12.9	1.9
$GlueVaR_{99.5\%,95\%}^{1/20,2/8}$	4.9	2.9	1.1	10.2	−1.3

[*] Benefit of diversification.

Next, a capital allocation application is illustrated where total capital has to be allocated between the three units of risk, X_1, X_2 and X_3. Table 7.2 shows particular allocation solutions for two proportional risk capital allocation principles using GlueVaR.

A different pattern is observed for the three GlueVaR risk measures when the stand-alone criterion or the partial contribution criterion is considered. In the case of the stand-alone criterion, the capital is allocated primarily to risk X_1, followed by X_2 and X_3, respectively. Let us focus on capital allocation solutions involving the partial contribution criterion in which confidence levels α_j, $j = 1, 2, 3$, are not forced to be equal across the risk units. A notable increase in the risk allocated to X_2 is observed if a partial contribution criterion with no constant level α_j and $GlueVaR_{99.5\%,95\%}^{1/20,2/8}$ is chosen[1]. This result is obtained because the impact on the quantile of X_2 is the opposite of that on X_1 and X_3 when α_j, $j = 1, 2, 3$, are estimated as F_S^{-1} $(95\%) = F_{X_1}^{-1}(\alpha_1) + F_{X_2}^{-1}(\alpha_2) + F_{X_3}^{-1}(\alpha_3)$. These confidence levels are equal to $\alpha_1 = 26\%$, $\alpha_2 = 98\%$ and $\alpha_3 = 43\%$. So, the associated quantiles for individual variables are $VaR_{26\%}(X_1)$, $VaR_{98\%}(X_2)$ and $VaR_{43\%}(X_3)$. The risk contribution of X_1 and X_3 are underweighted compared to the risk contribution of X_2. If we interpret the GlueVaR risk measure as a linear combina-

[1] The partial contribution criterion with constant level is not calculated in this example. However, there is a $\alpha^* = 95,42\%$ such that $VaR_{95\%}(Z) \simeq \sum_{j=1}^{3} VaR_{95,42\%}(X_j)$.

Table 7.2   Proportional capital allocation solutions using GlueVaR for the claim costs data

	Proportion allocated to X_1	Proportion allocated to X_2	Proportion allocated to X_3
Stand-alone criterion			
$\text{GlueVaR}_{99.5\%,95\%}^{11/30,2/3}$	50.41%	45.80%	3.79%
$\text{GlueVaR}_{99.5\%,95\%}^{0,1}$	63.51%	28.38%	8.11%
$\text{GlueVaR}_{99.5\%,95\%}^{1/20,1/8}$	54.44%	32.22%	12.22%
Partial contribution criterion with non constant $^{(a)}$ α_j			
$\text{GlueVaR}_{99.5\%,95\%}^{11/30,2/3}$ $^{(b)}$	46.42%	51.74%	1.84%
$\text{GlueVaR}_{99.5\%,95\%}^{0,1}$ $^{(b)}$	68.19%	26.86%	4.95%
$\text{GlueVaR}_{99.5\%,95\%}^{1/20,1/8}$ $^{(b)}$	25.11%	73.11%	2.78%

$^{(a)}$ Confidence levels $\alpha_j \in (0,1)$ are selected to satisfy $F_S^{-1}(95\%) = F_{X_1}^{-1}(\alpha_1) + F_{X_2}^{-1}(\alpha_2) + F_{X_3}^{-1}(\alpha_3)$. In this case $\alpha_1 = 26\%$, $\alpha_2 = 98\%$ and $\alpha_3 = 43\%$.

tion of $\omega_1 \cdot \text{TVaR}_{99.5\%} + \omega_2 \cdot \text{TVaR}_{95\%} + \omega_3 \cdot \text{VaR}_{95\%}$, the associated weights of the $\text{GlueVaR}_{99.5\%,95\%}^{1/20,2/8}$ are $\omega_1 = 1/24$, $\omega_2 = 1/12$ and $\omega_3 = 21/24$. So, the $\text{GlueVaR}_{99.5\%,95\%}^{1/20,1/8}$ reflects a risk measurement attitude just a bit more conservative than $\text{VaR}_{95\%}$, giving the largest weight to this risk value. Bearing in mind the quantitative tools that we have proposed in Chapter 5 to assess aggregate risk attitudes, the latter statement is reinforced by the following fact: the area under the distortion function of $\text{GlueVaR}_{99.5\%,95\%}^{1/20,2/8}$ is

$$\frac{1}{24} \cdot \frac{1+99.5\%}{2} + \frac{1}{12} \cdot \frac{1+95\%}{2} + \frac{21}{24} \cdot 95\% = 0.042 + 0.081 + 0.831$$
$$= 95.4\%$$

which is, effectively, slightly higher than 95%, the size of the area associated to $\text{VaR}_{95\%}$.

7.5   Exercices

1. Consider two risks that are Normally distributed with means, μ_1 and μ_2, both non-negative and covariance matrix S. Write a program to implement the GlueVaR stand-alone allocation principle assuming that the inputs are the distribution parameters and, in addition, α, β, ω_1, ω_2 and ω_3.

2. Assume n random variables, each one is uniformly distributed in the interval $[0, 100]$. Consider the GlueVaR stand-alone allocation principle, where $\omega_1 = \omega_2 = \omega_3$, express the result of the allocation to each component in terms of n, α and β.

3. Assume n random variables, each one is uniformly distributed in the interval $[0, 100]$. Consider the GlueVaR stand-alone allocation principle, where $\alpha = 0.95$ and $\beta = 0.99$, express the result of the allocation to each component in terms of n, ω_1, ω_2 and ω_3 and discuss the particular cases when $\omega_1 = 1$ or $\omega_2 = 1$.

4. Consider the example described in Section 7.4 and consider a change of monetary units, which means that each variable is multiplied by a constant $E > 0$, where E is the exchange rate. How would that modification affect the capital allocation results if nothing else changes?

8 Capital allocation principles as compositional data

In Chapter 6 it was shown that given an (absolute) capital allocation principle $\vec{K}$ with $K = \sum_{j=1}^{n} K_j$, its relative counterpart is defined as $\vec{x}$, where components are $x_i = K_i / K$. This chapter is devoted to show that relative capital allocation principles can be understood as belonging to the (standard) simplex. Following a nomenclature often used by geologists, any vector of the simplex is called a *composition* and any set of vectors in the simplex is called *compositional data*. This chapter first presents the metric space structure of the simplex. Secondly, it is shown that it is possible to move forward and backwards from relative capital allocation principles to compositions and the opposite. Applications of this relationship are illustrated with the data set used all along this book. This chapter is based on the study that we carried out in Belles-Sampera *et al.* [2016a].

8.1 The simplex and its vectorial and metric structure

Let us define the (standard) simplex $\mathscr{S}^n = \{\vec{z} \in \mathbb{R}^n \mid z_j \geqslant 0, \ j = 1, \dots, n, \ \sum_{j=1}^{n} z_j = 1\}$ provided with a particular structure of vector and metric space. Any vector $\vec{z} \in \mathscr{S}^n$ is a *composition* and a set of vectors is called *compositional data*. We need to define the vector space and to enrich it later with a distance in order to be allowed to talk about this vector space as a metric space. Any set of vectors needs two operations (often called vector addition and scalar multiplication) in order to be called a vector space over $\mathbb{R}$. These operations must satisfy a set of particular properties. The vector addition must be commutative, associative, and a neutral element is needed. Moreover, for each vector, its additive inverse must exist. A scalar multiplication for a vector space over $\mathbb{R}$ combines a real number with a vector and, whatever this combination is, it is necessary that the combination must belong again to the set of vectors. Additionally, a neutral element for the scalar multiplication must exist, and the distributivity of the scalar multiplication with respect to the vector addition and, on the other side, the distributivity of the vector addition with respect to the scalar multiplication must be both satisfied.

Following the notation provided in Aitchison and Egozcue [2005], a vector addition called *perturbation* (denoted by $\oplus$) and a scalar multiplication called *powering* (denoted by $\odot$) may be attached to the set $\mathscr{S}^n$. These operations are defined by expressions (8.1) and (8.2), respectively, where $\vec{x}, \vec{y} \in \mathscr{S}^n$ and $\lambda \in \mathbb{R}$:

$$\vec{x} \oplus \vec{y} = \left(\frac{x_1 \cdot y_1}{\sum_{j=1}^{n} x_j \cdot y_j}, \ldots, \frac{x_n \cdot y_n}{\sum_{j=1}^{n} x_j \cdot y_j} \right), \tag{8.1}$$

$$\lambda \odot \vec{x} = \left(\frac{x_1^\lambda}{\sum_{j=1}^{n} x_j^\lambda}, \ldots, \frac{x_n^\lambda}{\sum_{j=1}^{n} x_j^\lambda} \right). \tag{8.2}$$

It can be proved that the simplex $\mathscr{S}^n$ provided with operations $\oplus$ and $\odot$ has a linear vector space structure of dimension $n-1$. An important function in the context of compositional data is the *closure function*, $\mathscr{C}$. The closure function applied to a vector in $\mathbb{R}^n$ returns another vector whose components are the components of the original vector divided by the sum of all the components of the original vector. Keeping this in mind, the following expressions hold:

$$\vec{x} \oplus \vec{y} = \mathscr{C}\left[(x_1 \cdot y_1, \ldots, x_n \cdot y_n) \right], \quad \lambda \odot \vec{x} = \mathscr{C}\left[\left(x_1^\lambda, \ldots, x_n^\lambda \right) \right].$$

Moreover, assuming the vector space structure of $(\mathscr{S}^n, \oplus, \odot)$, the neutral element $\vec{0}$ of $\oplus$ can be deduced. Given a vector $\vec{x}$ such that $x_i > 0$ for all i, the relationship $\vec{x} \oplus \vec{r} = \vec{0}$ informs that $\vec{r}$ is the inverse of $\vec{x}$ with respect to the perturbation operation, so it should be written as $\vec{r} = (-1) \odot \vec{x}$. In other words,

$$\vec{r} = \left(\frac{1/x_1}{\sum_{j=1}^{n} (1/x_j)}, \ldots, \frac{1/x_n}{\sum_{j=1}^{n} (1/x_j)} \right).$$

Then, using this last expression and (8.1),

$$\vec{0} = \vec{x} \oplus \vec{r} = \mathscr{C}\left[\left(\frac{1}{\sum_{j=1}^{n} (1/x_j)}, \ldots, \frac{1}{\sum_{j=1}^{n} (1/x_j)} \right) \right] = \left(\frac{1}{n}, \ldots, \frac{1}{n} \right),$$

so the neutral element $\vec{0}$ of the perturbation operation is the composition with all of its n elements equal to $1/n$.

Figure 8.1   Example of perturbation (addition) and powering (scalar multiplication) in $\mathscr{S}^2$

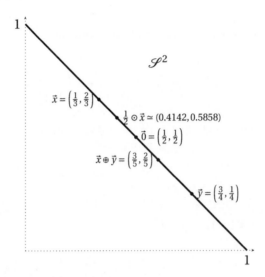

Example 8.1 (Perturbation, powering and neutral element in $\mathscr{S}^2$). We provide an example in a low dimension ($n = 2$) in order to illustrate how the vector spaces ($\mathscr{S}^n$, $\oplus$, $\odot$) work. Consider $\vec{x} = (1/3, 2/3)$ and $\vec{y} = (3/4, 1/4)$ in $\mathscr{S}^2$, and $\lambda = 1/2 \in \mathbb{R}$. We can ask ourselves for $\vec{x} \oplus \vec{y}$, $\lambda \odot \vec{x}$ and $\vec{0}$

$$\vec{x} \oplus \vec{y} = \left(\frac{1}{4}\frac{5}{12}, \frac{1}{6}\frac{5}{12} \right) = \left(\frac{3}{5}, \frac{2}{5} \right),$$

$$\lambda \odot \vec{x} = \left(\frac{\sqrt{1/3}}{\sqrt{1/3} + \sqrt{2/3}}, \frac{\sqrt{2/3}}{\sqrt{1/3} + \sqrt{2/3}} \right) \simeq (0.4142, 0.5858) , \text{ and}$$

$$\vec{0} = \left(\frac{1}{2}, \frac{1}{2} \right).$$

For instance, $\vec{x} \oplus \vec{0} = \left(\frac{1}{6}\frac{1}{2}, \frac{1}{3}\frac{1}{2} \right) = \left(\frac{1}{3}, \frac{2}{3} \right) = \vec{x}.$

All these vectors are displayed in Figure 8.1.

Finally, a distance is needed in order to consider the vector space ($\mathscr{S}^n$, $\oplus$, $\odot$) as a metric space. The *simplicial metric* defined in Aitchison [1983] is here considered. Given two compositions $\vec{x}$, $\vec{y}$, the distance between them from the point of view of the simplicial metric is

$$\Delta(\vec{x}, \vec{y}) = \left[\sum_{i=1}^{n} \left[\ln\left(\frac{x_i}{\mathrm{GM}(\vec{x})} \right) - \ln\left(\frac{y_i}{\mathrm{GM}(\vec{y})} \right) \right]^2 \right]^{1/2}, \tag{8.3}$$

where $\mathrm{GM}(\vec{z})$ denotes the geometric mean of the components of $\vec{z}$ vector, this is $\mathrm{GM}(\vec{z}) = \left[\prod_{i=1}^{n} z_i\right]^{1/n}$.

An equivalent expression for $\Delta(\vec{x}, \vec{y})$ is the following:

$$\Delta(\vec{x}, \vec{y}) = \left[\frac{1}{2n}\sum_{i=1}^{n}\sum_{j=1}^{n}\left[\ln\left(\frac{x_i}{x_j}\right) - \ln\left(\frac{y_i}{y_j}\right)\right]^2\right]^{1/2}. \qquad (8.4)$$

This simplicial metric is linked to a norm $\|\cdot\|_\Delta$ and to an inner product $\langle,\rangle_\Delta$ in a usual way. Given two vectors $\vec{x}$, $\vec{y} \in \mathcal{S}^n$,

$$\Delta(\vec{x}, \vec{y}) = \|\vec{x} \ominus \vec{y}\|_\Delta = \sqrt{\langle \vec{x} \ominus \vec{y}, \vec{x} \ominus \vec{y}\rangle_\Delta},$$

where $\vec{x} \ominus \vec{y} = \vec{x} \oplus [(-1) \odot \vec{y}]$, and

$$\langle \vec{u}, \vec{v}\rangle_\Delta = \frac{1}{2n}\sum_{i=1}^{n}\sum_{j=1}^{n}\left[\ln\left(\frac{u_i}{u_j}\right) \cdot \ln\left(\frac{v_i}{v_j}\right)\right]. \qquad (8.5)$$

Example 8.2 (Level curves in $\mathcal{S}^3$). Once the distances are defined, we can explore – for instance – the geometrical locus of all those elements in the simplex with the same distance to a given element in that simplex. In other words, we could be interested in determining a sort of *level curves* in $\mathcal{S}^n$ related to the distances of compositions $\vec{x} \in \mathcal{S}^n$ to a fixed composition $\vec{y}_0$. Each one of these level curves would be driven by a certain $d \in \mathbb{R}^+$, the target distance. Formally, we could look for geometrical loci denoted $\mathrm{lc}_d(\vec{y}_0)$ and defined by

$$\mathrm{lc}_d(\vec{y}_0) = \{\vec{x} \in \mathcal{S}^n \mid \Delta(\vec{x}, \vec{y}_0) = d\}.$$

In Figure 8.2 several level curves are represented in a two dimensional projection of $\mathcal{S}^3$. On the left, $\mathrm{lc}_d(\vec{0})$ for $d = 0.2$, 0.45, 0.8 and 1.0 are represented. As it is observed, the higher the distance to the composition of reference (in this case, $\vec{y}_0 = \vec{0} = (1/3, 1/3, 1/3)$) the sharper the curve. Differences with respect to the Euclidean distance are evident, because these level curves have not circular shapes with center in the composition of reference. The behavior is similar on the right hand side of Figure 8.2. In that case, the composition of reference is $\vec{y}_0 = (1/8, 1/2, 3/8)$ instead of the neutral element with respect to the perturbation (addition). The corresponding level curves $\mathrm{lc}_d(\vec{y}_0)$ for $d = 0.2$, 0.45, 0.8 and 1.0 are once again represented but with this alternative reference.

Figure 8.2 **Examples of *level curves* $\mathrm{lc}_d(\vec{y}_0)$ in $\mathscr{S}^3$ are displayed. In fact, they are projections in $\mathbb{R}^2$ of the geometrical loci $\mathrm{lc}_d(\vec{y}_0)$ of the elements which distances to point $\vec{y}_0$ are equal to d, where $d = 0.2$, $d = 0.45$, $d = 0.8$ and $d = 1.0$.**
***Left figure:** $\vec{y}_0 = (1/3, 1/3, 1/3)$ (neutral element with respect to the perturbation).*
***Right figure:** $\vec{y}_0 = (1/8, 1/2, 3/8)$.*

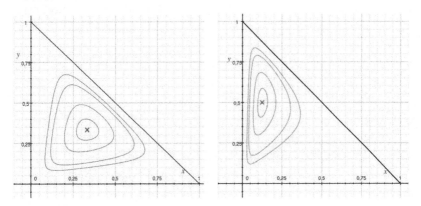

Under this framework, as it was shown in De Baets [2013], the *simplicial arithmetic mean* of the compositional data $\vec{x}_1, \vec{x}_2, \ldots, \vec{x}_m$ may be understood as a solution of a minimization problem, in the following way:

$$\mathrm{AM}_\Delta(\vec{x}_1, \ldots, \vec{x}_m) = \frac{1}{m} \odot \bigoplus_{k=1}^{m} \vec{x}_k = \arg\min_{\vec{z}} \sum_{k=1}^{m} \|\vec{z} \ominus \vec{x}_k\|_\Delta^2, \qquad (8.6)$$

where $\bigoplus_{k=1}^{m} \vec{x}_k$ means the perturbation of the set of m compositions $\{\vec{x}_k\}_{k=1,\ldots,m}$. At first sight, this expression is equivalent to the arithmetic mean of m real numbers $u_1, u_2, \ldots, u_m$:

$$\mathrm{AM}(u_1, \ldots, u_m) = \frac{1}{m} \cdot \sum_{k=1}^{m} u_k = \arg\min_{v} \sum_{k=1}^{m} \|v - u_k\|_2^2, \qquad (8.7)$$

so, the simplicial metric presented in this section is the natural metric choice if (simplicial) arithmetic means are computed. In other words, the expression (8.6) contains the proper definition of the arithmetic mean of $\vec{x}_1, \ldots, \vec{x}_m$ in the metric space $(\mathscr{S}^n, \oplus, \odot, \Delta)$. From the definitions of both perturbation and powering operations, an explicit expression for the simplicial arithmetic mean presented in (8.6) is

$$\mathrm{AM}_\Delta(\vec{x}_1, \ldots, \vec{x}_m) = \mathscr{C}[(G_1, \ldots, G_n)], \qquad (8.8)$$

where $G_k = GM(x_{1,k}, x_{2,k}, \ldots, x_{m,k})$, i.e. $G_k = \left[\prod_{i=1}^{m} x_{i,k}\right]^{1/m}$, for all $k = 1, \ldots, n$.

8.1.1 From capital allocation principles to compositional data

An absolute capital allocation $\vec{K}$ has its relative counterpart $\vec{x}$ computed as $x_i = K_i/K$ for all $i = 1, \ldots, n$. Note that it is satisfied that $\sum_{j=1}^{n} x_j = 1$. Note also that when negative allocated capital amounts K_i are allowed, the relative components would be negative and then $\vec{x} \notin \mathscr{S}^n$. For the rest of the chapter it is assumed that $\vec{x}$ has strictly positive components. That is, we assume that $\vec{x}$ is a composition with non-zero and non-negative components. This assumption allows to avoid negative or zero values on components of $\vec{x}$, which are an inconvenient for practitioners (negative allocations) and when operating in the simplex (null compositions)[1].

At this point, some concepts introduced in Chapter 6 to classify absolute capital allocation problems can be associated to concepts introduced in this chapter. For instance, if we consider proportional capital allocation principles as stated in expression (6.1), the relative counterpart $\vec{y}$ of the absolute principle $\vec{K} = (K_1, \ldots, K_n)$ may be interpreted as the closure of the vector with components equal to $f_i(X_i)$, $i = 1, \ldots, n$:

$$\vec{K} \text{ s.t. } K_i = K \cdot \frac{f_i(X_i)}{\sum\limits_{j=1}^{n} f_j(X_j)}, \ \forall\, i = 1, \ldots, n \qquad (8.9)$$
$$\Leftrightarrow \vec{y} = \mathscr{C}\left[(f_1(X_1), \ldots, f_n(X_n))\right].$$

When stand-alone proportional principles are considered, the previous expression helps to visualize why dependence structures between random variables $\{X_i\}_{i=1,\ldots,n}$ are not taken at all into account in the capital allocation solution. In a first step, the amount of risk faced by each agent is assigned to one of them, which is summarized by $f_i(X_i)$, $i = 1, \ldots, n$. Subsequently, the relative risk proportion obtained in that manner is scaled by K to obtain the final capital allocation.

8.2 Perturbation inverse, simplicial distance and simplicial arithmetic mean applied to capital allocation problems

In the previous section, it has been shown that relative capital allocation principles and compositions may be naturally linked. Once this relationship

---

[1] Although elements of a composition can be equal to zero, dealing with compositions with null components is not an easy task in practice.

is established, the idea is to take advantage of the geometric structure of the simplex to enrich the description of each capital allocation principle and each capital allocation result. Some applications of compositional methods in the context of capital allocation problems are shown in this section.

8.2.1 The inverse of a capital allocation

Let us consider a relative capital allocation principle $\vec{x}$ linked to what we have called in Chapter 6 a cost of risk goal. A manager would want to depart from this allocation to distribute rewards instead of costs in order to fulfill an allocation with a reward to an objective linked to minimisation of risk. An intuitive idea is to invert each of the relative components, in order to reflect the inverse nature of the allocation (a relative low cost allocated to ith agent should mean a relative high reward assigned to him). To proceed in this direction, one must normalize the sum of all $1/x_i$ in order to provide a full allocation of the whole amount of capital, K. Note that the inversion of the components is only feasible if all components of $\vec{x}$ are different from 0. This application has a natural interpretation in the simplex $\mathscr{S}^n$. The normalization can be understood as the application of the closure function. Given a relative capital allocation principle $\vec{x}$, let $\vec{r}$ be the closure of the vector with components $1/x_i$ for $i = 1, \ldots, n$. As it has been shown in Section 8.1, $\vec{r}$ is the inverse of $\vec{x}$ with respect to the perturbation operation: $\vec{r} = (-1) \odot \vec{x}$.

Using risk based capital allocation principles to determine penalizations or rewards may lead to undesirable behaviors of the agents. Basically, agents have incentives to take conservative business decisions because less risk results in a better reward. In order to prevent it, a return-on-risk measure seems to be preferable to assign rewards. It has been indicated in Chapter 6 that rewards on *risk and return* allocations may be of great relevance for a sound ERM system.

Note now that there are some direct absolute reward on *risk and return* capital allocation principles that can be considered. For instance, if we depart from a given $\vec{x} = \mathscr{C}[\vec{y}]$, where $y_i = \mathrm{RORAC}(X_i \mid S)/\mathrm{RORAC}(S)$, for all $i = 1, \ldots, n$.

Then, we obtain the absolute capital allocation principle $\vec{K}$ by

$$K_i = K \cdot x_i = K \cdot \frac{\mathrm{RORAC}(X_i \mid S)}{\sum_{j=1}^{n} \mathrm{RORAC}(X_j \mid S)}, \quad \forall i = 1, \ldots, n.$$

The underlying idea is to give a higher reward to those agents whose relative RORAC with respect to the overall RORAC of the portfolio is higher.

Note that different definitions of return-on-risk measures than expressions (6.3) and (6.2) in Chapter 6 for RORAC($X_i \mid S$) and RORAC(S) may be considered, and the objective of the allocation would not change.

8.2.2   Ranking capital allocation principles

We have presented a simplicial metric or distance Δ which helps to constitute $\mathscr{S}^n$ as a metric space. Δ can be used to quantitatively rank capital allocation principles. Let us consider the neutral composition $\vec{0} \in \mathscr{S}^n$ which is the composition with all of its n components equal to $1/n$. So, the distance between any relative capital allocation principle $\vec{x}$ and $\vec{0}$ can be computed. Alternatively, the distance between any pair of relative capital allocation principles belonging to $\mathscr{S}^n$ can be calculated. Both uses of the simplicial distance are useful to compare different capital allocation principles in a quantitative manner.

When the distance between the relative capital allocation $\vec{x}$ and $\vec{0}$ is computed, a quantitative result shows how far the allocation principle is from a neutral assignment. Note that $\vec{0} \in \mathscr{S}^n$ is linked to a capital allocation principle in which no matter how much risk each agent faces, they would all receive the same since the same amount is allocated to each one (K/n). On the other hand, if an allocation principle is taken as a reference (for instance, a gradient allocation principle as explained in Section 6.3.1 of Chapter 6), the distance between the composition linked to this principle and any other composition quantifies how far this principle is from the allocation of reference.

Imagine that four allocation principles are in hand for the same amount K of money and the same n agents: a haircut allocation principle (7.2), $\vec{K}_h$; a covariance allocation principle (6.15), $\vec{K}_c$; a stand-alone proportional allocation principle based on GlueVaR (7.5), $\vec{K}_s$; and a gradient allocation principle related to (6.5), $\vec{K}_g$. If their respective relative allocation principles $\vec{x}_h$, $\vec{x}_c$, $\vec{x}_s$ and $\vec{x}_g$ are in $\mathscr{S}^n$ and each of the components of $\vec{x}_t$, $t \in \{h, c, s, g\}$ is strictly positive, then it is possible to rank them in two different ways:

1) Compute $\Delta(\vec{x}_t, \vec{0})$ for $t \in \{h, c, s, g\}$. Order distances in an increasing order. A higher order position indicates an allocation located further apart from the neutral allocation;

2) Choose one of the principles as reference (for instance, the gradient allocation principle). Compute $\Delta\left(\vec{x}_t, \vec{x}_g\right)$ for $t \in \{h, c, s\}$. These three values are quantifying how far each principle is from the allocation of reference.

8.2.3 Averaging capital allocation principles

In practice, different management teams may suggest different capital allocations regarding the same assignment problem. The situation sketched at the end of the previous section could be an example of such a situation. In those cases, we want to stress that the set of different capital allocation principles can be aggregated through the simplicial arithmetic mean, obtaining a final allocation that considers each one of the available viewpoints.

Formally, let us imagine m management teams providing m absolute capital allocation principles $\vec{K}_k$ of amount K to the same n agents, and let $\vec{x}_k$ be the relative capital allocation principles linked to $\vec{K}_k$, $k = 1,\dots,m$. Once again, taking advantage of the geometric structure of $\mathscr{S}^n$, the concept of *averaging* the m points of view on the same allocation problem is easily derived. In other words, the expression $\vec{z} = \mathrm{AM}_\Delta(\vec{x}_1,\dots,\vec{x}_m)$ is the proper definition of the arithmetic mean of $\vec{x}_1,\dots,\vec{x}_m$ in the metric space $(\mathscr{S}^n, \oplus, \odot, \Delta)$ as it was shown in (8.6). Once the relative arithmetic mean is obtained, what remains to do is to assign an amount of $\bar{K}_i = K \cdot z_i$ monetary units to each ith agent, $i = 1,\dots,n$, in order to provide a capital allocation principle in the adequate scale. This principle balances the opinions of all the involved management teams.

8.2.4 An illustration

In order to illustrate the applications described in this section we are getting back to the relative principles obtained in Chapter 7, which where displayed in Table 7.2. Recall that these relative principles were derived from six absolute proportional allocation principles (6.1) based on three different GlueVaR risk measures but with two different perspectives: on the one hand, stand-alone proportional allocation principles (7.5) and, on the other hand, partial contributions based proportional allocation principles (7.9). Let us name them as $\vec{x}_i$, $i = 1,\dots,6$. Then

$$
\begin{aligned}
\vec{x}_1 &= (50.41\%, 45.80\%, 3.79\%), \\
\vec{x}_2 &= (63.51\%, 28.38\%, 8.11\%), \\
\vec{x}_3 &= (54.44\%, 32.22\%, 12.22\%), \\
\vec{x}_4 &= (46.42\%, 51.74\%, 1.84\%), \\
\vec{x}_5 &= (68.19\%, 26.86\%, 4.95\%), \\
\vec{x}_6 &= (25.11\%, 73.11\%, 1.78\%).
\end{aligned}
\tag{8.10}
$$

Table 8.1   Perturbation inverse relative capital allocation principles.

	X_1	X_2	X_3
	Stand-alone		
$\vec{y}_1 = (-1) \odot \vec{x}_1$	6.50%	7.15%	86.35%
$\vec{y}_2 = (-1) \odot \vec{x}_2$	9.03%	20.22%	70.75%
$\vec{y}_3 = (-1) \odot \vec{x}_3$	14.00%	23.65%	62.35%
	Based on partial contributions		
$\vec{y}_4 = (-1) \odot \vec{x}_4$	3.68%	3.30%	93.02%
$\vec{y}_5 = (-1) \odot \vec{x}_5$	5.78%	14.67%	79.56%
$\vec{y}_6 = (-1) \odot \vec{x}_6$	6.48%	2.22%	91.30%

From $\vec{x}_1$ to $\vec{x}_3$ the results correspond to stand-alone proportional allocation principles and the rest may be understood as proportional allocation principles base on partial contributions. In addition, $\vec{x}_1$ and $\vec{x}_4$ are linked to $\text{GlueVaR}_{99.5\%,95\%}^{11/30,2/3}$, $\vec{x}_2$ and $\vec{x}_5$ to $\text{GlueVaR}_{99.5\%,95\%}^{0,1}$ and the remaining were calculated based on $\text{GlueVaR}_{99.5\%,95\%}^{1/20,1/8}$. Note that all these relative principles belong to the simplex $\mathscr{S}^3$ and have non-zero components.

Assume now that risk managers are interested in allocation principles with a reward to conservative objctives (meaning the smaller the risk figure the better the type of risk). However, the only available information (principles $\vec{x}_i, i = 1,\dots,6$) is a set of capital allocation principles with a cost of risk goal. The computation of the inverse of relative capital allocation principles can be useful in this context, in order to obtain principles driven by a reward to a risk minimization objective. So the perturbation inverses of relative capital allocation principles $\vec{x}_i, i = 1,\dots,6$, are shown in Table 8.1 and they are denoted as $\vec{y}_i, i = 1,\dots,6$.

Using the relative principles displayed in (8.10), relative allocation principles are ranked according to Section 8.2.2. As before, symbol $\vec{0}$ is used to refer to the neutral allocation. The following simplicial distances are calculated from expression (8.3):

$$\Delta(\vec{x}_1, \vec{0}) = \sqrt{0.8 + 0.637 + 2.865} = 2.074,$$
$$\Delta(\vec{x}_2, \vec{0}) = \sqrt{0.911 + 0.022 + 1.218} = 1.4669,$$
$$\Delta(\vec{x}_3, \vec{0}) = \sqrt{0.453 + 0.022 + 0.674} = 1.0719,$$
$$\Delta(\vec{x}_4, \vec{0}) = \sqrt{1.083 + 1.32 + 4.795} = 2.6831,$$
$$\Delta(\vec{x}_5, \vec{0}) = \sqrt{1.404 + 0.064 + 2.068} = 1.8803,$$
$$\Delta(\vec{x}_6, \vec{0}) = \sqrt{0.276 + 2.542 + 4.495} = 2.7045.$$

(8.11)

Figure 8.3   Distances between capital allocation principles.

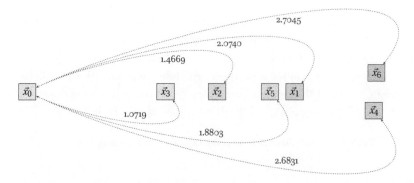

Distances considered individually are not too informative. However, these values allow to rank the principles with respect to one principle of reference, as it is graphically shown in Figure 8.3. From results (8.11), it can be deduced that, in this example, proportional allocation principles based on partial contributions are generally more distant from the neutral allocation than the rest (with $\vec{x}_1$ being the only exception). Additionally, when comparing pairs of compositions with the same risk measure involved, it becomes evident that the most different behavior is the one linked to principles depending on GlueVaR$_{99.5\%,95\%}^{1/20,1/8}$ risk measure (the pair $\vec{x}_3$ and $\vec{x}_6$). So, in this example, when using GlueVaR$_{99.5\%,95\%}^{1/20,1/8}$ as a risk measure, the selection of the allocation criterion (stand-alone versus based on partial contributions) seems to be more relevant than when using the other two GlueVaR risk measures under consideration.

As a final application, the three relative stand-alone allocations displayed in (8.10) are averaged by means of the simplicial arithmetic mean. The relative principles based on partial contributions are also averaged. Finally, the simplicial arithmetic mean of these previous averages is obtained, just for the sake of mixing both perspectives in one single principle following a hierarchical approach in which the *distribution criterion* (as mentioned in Section 6.1 of Chapter 6) plays an important role.

With respect to the stand-alone proportional allocation principles, the geometric means of the three components ($n = 3$) of the three ($m = 3$) relative capital allocations, denoted as G_1, G_2 and G_3, respectively, are computed. Their values are

$$G_1 = (50.41\% \cdot 63.51\% \cdot 54.44)^{1/3} = 55.86\%,$$

$$G_2 = (45.8\% \cdot 28.38\% \cdot 32.22)^{1/3} = 34.73\% \text{ and}$$

$$G_3 = (3.79\% \cdot 8.11\% \cdot 12.22)^{1/3} = 7.22\%.$$

Following expression (8.8), we calculate the value of $\mathscr{C}[(G_1, G_2, G_3)]$, i.e. the closure of the vector with components being the geometric means G_1, G_2 and G_3. By doing so, the value of the simplicial average $AM_\Delta(\vec{x}_1, \vec{x}_2, \vec{x}_3)$ is obtained which is a relative allocation principle. Similarly, the simplicial arithmetic mean of the relative principles based on partial contributions $AM_\Delta(\vec{x}_4, \vec{x}_5, \vec{x}_6)$ is also obtained. Both results are shown in Table 8.2.

Table 8.2   **Simplicial means of the capital allocation principles**

	X_1	X_2	X_3
$AM_\Delta(\vec{x}_1, \vec{x}_2, \vec{x}_3)$	57.11%	35.51%	7.38%
$AM_\Delta(\vec{x}_4, \vec{x}_5, \vec{x}_6)$	46.64%	50.60%	2.74%

As it can be proved, the components of the simplicial averages are not equal to the arithmetic mean of the components of the original principles. In fact, the components of the simplicial average are linked to the geometric mean of the components of the original relative principles. As a final result, let us average the two principles displayed in Table 8.2. In this case, the geometric means of the three components ($n = 3$) of the two ($m = 2$) relative capital allocations, denoted as G_1', G_2' and G_3', respectively, are computed. Their values are

$$G_1' = \sqrt{57.11\% \cdot 46.64\%} = 51.61\%,$$

$$G_2' = \sqrt{35.51\% \cdot 50.62\%} = 42.39\% \text{ and}$$
$$G_3' = \sqrt{7.38\% \cdot 2.74\%} = 4.5\%.$$

In order to obtain the final result, we need to calculate the closure of $\vec{w} = (G_1', G_2', G_3')$. This is

$$\text{AM}_\Delta \left(\text{AM}_\Delta(\vec{x}_1, \vec{x}_2, \vec{x}_3), \text{AM}_\Delta(\vec{x}_4, \vec{x}_5, \vec{x}_6) \right) = \mathscr{C}[\vec{w}].$$

This relative principle is

$$(52.40\%, 43.04\%, 4.57\%).$$

Final remark. Another feasible approach to reach this unique allocation would be to calculate the simplicial arithmetic mean of the whole set of relative principles shown in (8.10). It has to be noted that the result would certainly be different, because this last approach would lack the specific aggregation hierarchy that we have imposed herein.

8.3 Exercises

1. In the example presented in Section 8.2.4, calculate the simplicial distance between $\text{AM}_\Delta \left(\text{AM}_\Delta(\vec{x}_1, \vec{x}_2, \vec{x}_3), \text{AM}_\Delta(\vec{x}_4, \vec{x}_5, \vec{x}_6) \right)$ and $\text{AM}_\Delta (\vec{x}_1, \vec{x}_2, \vec{x}_3, \vec{x}_4, \vec{x}_5, \vec{x}_6)$ where $\vec{x}_i$, $i = 1, \ldots, 6$, are the relative principles shown in (8.10).

2. Observe the distances between principles shown in the example presented in Section 8.2.4, find a stand-alone allocation which is located between $\vec{x}_1$ and $\vec{x}_2$.

3. Assume an allocation principle in a situation of n different sources that assigns an allocation equal to $2i/(n(n+1))$ for the risk i, $i = 1, \ldots, n$. Show that this is not the neutral allocation and find the distance to this element as a function of n. Calculate the behaviour of this distance as n increases.

4. In the same situation as in the previous exercise, propose another allocation for i, $i = 1, \ldots, n$, different to the neutral allocation and compare it to $2i/(n(n+1))$ for the risk i, $i = 1, \ldots, n$.

5. Assume a situation of n different sources that assigns an allocation equal to $2i/(n(n+1))$ for the risk i, $i = 1, \ldots, n$, find an average allocation that

summarizes the allocations provided by this one and the neutral allocation. Find the average allocation now also with the third allocation that
you proposed in the previous exercise.

Appendix A

A.1 Equivalent expression for the GlueVaR distortion function

Details on the definition of the GlueVaR distortion function $\kappa_{\beta,\alpha}^{h_1,h_2}(u)$ as a linear combination of the distortion functions of TVaR at confidence levels β and α, and VaR at confidence level α are provided, i.e. an explanation of how to obtain expression (3.3) can be found here. Expression (3.1) of the distortion function $\kappa_{\beta,\alpha}^{h_1,h_2}(u)$ can be rewritten as,

$$\kappa_{\beta,\alpha}^{h_1,h_2}(u) = h_1 \cdot \gamma_\beta(u) \cdot \mathbb{1}[0 \leqslant u < 1 - \beta]$$
$$+ \left(h_1 + \frac{h_2 - h_1}{\beta - \alpha} \cdot (1 - \alpha) \cdot \gamma_\alpha(u) - \frac{h_2 - h_1}{\beta - \alpha} \cdot (1 - \beta) \right) \cdot$$
$$\mathbb{1}[1 - \beta \leqslant u < 1 - \alpha] + \psi_\alpha(u), \tag{A.1}$$

where $\mathbb{1}[x_1 \leqslant u < x_2]$ is an indicator function, so it takes a value of 1 if $u \in [x_1, x_2]$ and 0 otherwise.

Note that

$$\gamma_\beta(u) \cdot \mathbb{1}[0 \leqslant u < 1 - \beta] = \gamma_\beta(u) - \psi_\beta(u), \tag{A.2}$$

$$\mathbb{1}[1 - \beta \leqslant u < 1 - \alpha] = \psi_\beta(u) - \psi_\alpha(u), \tag{A.3}$$

$$\gamma_\alpha(u) \cdot \mathbb{1}[1 - \beta \leqslant u < 1 - \alpha] =$$
$$\gamma_\alpha(u) - \psi_\alpha(u) - \left(\frac{1 - \beta}{1 - \alpha} \right) \cdot [\gamma_\beta(u) - \psi_\beta(u)]. \tag{A.4}$$

Taking into account expressions (A.2), (A.3) and (A.4), expression (A.1) may be rewritten as,

$$\kappa_{\beta,\alpha}^{h_1,h_2}(u) = \left[h_1 - \frac{(h_2 - h_1) \cdot (1 - \beta)}{\beta - \alpha} \right] \cdot \gamma_\beta(u) +$$

$$\left[-h_1 + h_1 - \frac{(h_2 - h_1) \cdot (1 - \beta)}{\beta - \alpha} + \frac{(h_2 - h_1) \cdot (1 - \beta)}{\beta - \alpha} \right] \cdot \psi_\beta(u) +$$

$$\frac{h_2 - h_1}{\beta - \alpha} \cdot (1 - \alpha) \cdot \gamma_\alpha(u) + \tag{A.5}$$

$$\left[1 - h_1 + \frac{(h_2 - h_1) \cdot (1 - \beta)}{\beta - \alpha} - \frac{h_2 - h_1}{\beta - \alpha} \cdot (1 - \alpha) \right] \cdot \psi_\alpha(u).$$

Given that $\omega_1 = h_1 - \dfrac{(h_2 - h_1) \cdot (1 - \beta)}{\beta - \alpha}$, $\omega_2 = \dfrac{h_2 - h_1}{\beta - \alpha} \cdot (1 - \alpha)$ and $\omega_3 = 1 - h_2$, expression (3.3) follows directly from (A.5). $\qquad\square$

A.2   Bijective relationship between heights and weights as parameters for GlueVaR risk measures

Pairs of GlueVaR heights (h_1, h_2) and weights (ω_1, ω_2) are linearly related to each other. The parameter relationships are $(h_1, h_2)' = H \cdot (\omega_1, \omega_2)'$ and, inversely, $(\omega_1, \omega_2)' = H^{-1} \cdot (h_1, h_2)'$, where H and H^{-1} matrices are $H =$

$$\begin{pmatrix} 1 & \dfrac{1 - \beta}{1 - \alpha} \\ 1 & 1 \end{pmatrix} \text{ and } H^{-1} = \begin{pmatrix} \dfrac{1 - \alpha}{\beta - \alpha} & \dfrac{\beta - 1}{\beta - \alpha} \\ \dfrac{\alpha - 1}{\beta - \alpha} & \dfrac{1 - \alpha}{\beta - \alpha} \end{pmatrix}, \text{ respectively.}$$

A.3   Relationship between GlueVaR and Tail Distortion risk measures

This section of the appendix is intended to present the proof of Proposition 4.1. Following the notation introduced along this work, as for any random variable X it holds that $\text{GlueVaR}_{\beta,\alpha}^{\omega_1,\omega_2}(X) = \int X d\mu$ with $\mu = \kappa_{\beta,\alpha}^{\omega_1,\omega_2} \circ P$ and $T_{g,\alpha}(X) = \int X d\eta$ with $\eta = g_\alpha \circ P$, proving Proposition 4.1 is equivalent to proving that $\kappa_{\beta,\alpha}^{\omega_1,\omega_2} = g_\alpha$ under the proper conditions on ω_1, ω_2 and g.
On one hand, suppose that $\omega_2 = 1 - \omega_1$ and that g is given by expression (4.2). First of all, let us rewrite g as

$$g(t) = \left(\frac{\omega_1 \cdot (1 - \alpha)}{1 - \beta} + \omega_2 \right) \cdot t \cdot \mathbb{1}\left[0 \leq t < (1 - \alpha)^{-1} \cdot (1 - \beta) \right] +$$

$$(\omega_1 + \omega_2 \cdot t) \cdot \mathbb{1}\left[(1 - \alpha)^{-1} \cdot (1 - \beta) \leq t \leq 1 \right]$$

Recall that g_α is built as $g\left(\frac{u}{1-\alpha} \right) \cdot \mathbb{1}[0 \leq u < 1 - \alpha] + \mathbb{1}[1 - \alpha \leq u \leq 1]$. If u is less than $1 - \beta$ therefore $t = \frac{u}{1-\alpha}$ is less than $(1 - \alpha)^{-1} \cdot (1 - \beta)$; if u is comprised between $1 - \beta$ and $1 - \alpha$, then $t = \frac{u}{1-\alpha}$ satisfies that $(1 - \alpha)^{-1} \cdot (1 - \beta) \leq t \leq 1$. Summarizing,

$$
g_\alpha(u) = \begin{cases}
\left[\dfrac{\omega_1}{1 - \beta} + \dfrac{\omega_2}{1 - \alpha} \right] \cdot u & \text{if } 0 \leq u < 1 - \beta \\[2ex]
\omega_1 + \dfrac{\omega_2}{1 - \alpha} \cdot u & \text{if } 1 - \beta \leq u < 1 - \alpha \\[2ex]
1 & \text{if } 1 - \alpha \leq u \leq 1
\end{cases}
\tag{A.6}
$$

which is the definition of distortion function $\kappa_{\beta,\alpha}^{\omega_1,\omega_2}$ as shown in (3.5).

On the other hand, consider as starting point the aforementioned expression (3.5) of $\kappa_{\beta,\alpha}^{\omega_1,\omega_2}$. As pointed out, g_α is always continuous in $1 - \alpha$. Consequently parameters of $\kappa_{\beta,\alpha}^{\omega_1,\omega_2}$ must be such that guaranty continuity of the equivalent g_α in $1 - \alpha$. In other words, $\lim_{u \uparrow (1-\alpha)} \kappa_{\beta,\alpha}^{\omega_1,\omega_2}(u) = \omega_1 + \omega_2 = 1 = \lim_{u \downarrow (1-\alpha)} \kappa_{\beta,\alpha}^{\omega_1,\omega_2}(u)$. This is exactly condition $\omega_2 = 1 - \omega_1$. Now, forcing $g_\alpha = \kappa_{\beta,\alpha}^{\omega_1,\omega_2}$, it is straightforward to go backwards from expression (A.6) to expression (4.2) to complete the proof. $\square$

Bibliography

Acerbi, C. and Tasche, D. (2002). On the coherence of expected shortfall. *Journal of Banking & Finance*, 26 (7): 1487–1503.

Aggarwal, A., Beck, M., Cann, M., Ford, T., Georgescu, D., Morjaria, N., Smith, A., Taylor, Y., Tsanakas, A., Witts, L., *et al.* (2016). Model risk–daring to open up the black box. *British Actuarial Journal*, 21 (2): 229–296.

Aitchison, J. (1983). Principal component analysis of compositional data. *Biometrika*, 70 (1): 57–65.

Aitchison, J. and Egozcue, J. (2005). Compositional data analysis: Where are we and where should we be heading? *Mathematical Geology*, 37 (7): 829–850.

Alemany, R., Bolancé, C., and Guillen, M. (2013). A nonparametric approach to calculating value-at-risk. *Insurance: Mathematics and Economics*, 52: 255–262.

Alexander, C. and Sarabia, J. M. (2012). Quantile uncertainty and Value-at-Risk model risk. *Risk Analysis*, 32 (8): 1293–1308.

Artzner, P., Delbaen, F., Eber, J.-M., and Heath, D. (1999). Coherent measures of risk. *Mathematical Finance*, 9 (3): 203–228.

Asimit, A. V., Furman, E., Tang, Q., and Vernic, R. (2011). Asymptotics for risk capital allocations based on Conditional Tail Expectation. *Insurance: Mathematics and Economics*, 49 (3): 310–324.

Aven, T. (2012). Foundational issues in risk assessment and risk management. *Risk Analysis*, 32 (10): 1647–1656.

Aven, T. (2013). On the meaning and use of the risk appetite concept. *Risk Analysis*, 33 (3): 462–468.

Bahraoui, Z., Bolance, C., and Pérez-Marín, A. M. (2014). Testing extreme value copulas to estimate the quantile. *SORT: Statistics and Operations Research Transactions*, 27 (1): 89–102.

Balbás, A., Garrido, J., and Mayoral, S. (2009). Properties of distortion risk measures. *Methodology and Computing in Applied Probability*, 11 (3, SI): 385–399.

Balog, D. (2010). Risk based capital allocation. *In: Proceedings of FIKUSZ '10 Symposium for Young Researchers*, pages 17–26.

Belles-Sampera, J. (2011). Capital allocation and distortion risk measures. Master's thesis, Department of Econometrics - University of Barcelona.

Belles-Sampera, J., Guillen, M., and Santolino, M. (2013a). Generalizing some usual risk measures in financial and insurance applications. *In: Fernández-Izquierdo, M., Muñoz Torres, M., and León, R., editors, Modeling and Simulation in Engineering, Economics and Management. Proceedings of the MS 2013 International Conference*, volume 145 of *Lecture Notes in Business Information Processing*, pages 75–82. Springer-Verlag.

Belles-Sampera, J., Guillen, M., and Santolino, M. (2014a). Beyond Value-at-Risk: GlueVaR distortion risk measures. *Risk Analysis*, 34 (1): 121–134.

Belles-Sampera, J., Guillen, M., and Santolino, M. (2014b). GlueVaR risk measures in capital allocation applications. *Insurance: Mathematics and Economics*, 58: 132–137.

Belles-Sampera, J., Guillen, M., and Santolino, M. (2016a). Compositional methods applied to capital allocation problems. *Journal of Risk*. In press.

Belles-Sampera, J., Guillen, M., and Santolino, M. (2016b). The use of flexible quantile-based measures in risk assessment. *Communication in Statistics – Theory and Methods*, 45 (6): 1670–1681.

Belles-Sampera, J., Guillen, M., and Santolino, M. (2016c). What attitudes to risk underlie distortion risk measure choices? *Insurance: Mathematics and Economics*, 61: 101–109.

Belles-Sampera, J., Merigó, J. M., Guillen, M., and Santolino, M. (2013b). The connection between distortion risk measures and ordered weighted averaging operators. *Insurance: Mathematics and Economics*, 52 (2): 411–420.

Belles-Sampera, J., Merigó, J. M., Guillen, M., and Santolino, M. (2014c). Indicators for the characterization of discrete Choquet integrals. *Information Sciences*, 267: 201–216.

Belles-Sampera, J., Merigó, J. M., and Santolino, M. (2013c). Some new definitions of indicators for the Choquet integral. *In: H. Bustince, J. Fernández, T. Calvo and R. Mesiar, editor, Aggregation Functions in Theory and Practice. Proceedings of the 7th International Summer School on Aggregation Operators*, volume 228 of *Advances in Intelligent Systems and Soft Computing*, pages 467–476. Springer-Verlag.

Bellini, F. and Gianin, E. R. (2012). Haezendonck-Goovaerts risk measures and Orlicz quantiles. *Insurance: Mathematics and Economics*, 51 (1): 107–114.

Bellini, F., Klar, B., Mueller, A., and Gianin, E. R. (2014). Generalized quantiles as risk measures. *Insurance: Mathematics and Economics*, 54: 41–48.

Bleichrodt, H. and Eeckhoudt, L. (2006). Survival risks, intertemporal consumption, and insurance: The case of distorted probabilities. *Insurance: Mathematics and Economics*, 38 (2): 335–346.

Bolancé, C., Bahraoui, Z., and Artís, M. (2014). Quantifying the risk using copulae with nonparametric marginals. *Insurance: Mathematics and Economics*, 58: 46–56.

Bolancé, C., Guillen, M., Gustafsson, J., and Nielsen, J. P. (2012). Quantitative operational risk models.

Bolancé, C., Guillen, M., Gustafsson, J., and Nielsen, J. P. (2013). Adding prior knowledge to quantitative operational risk models. *Journal of Operationa Risk*, 8 (1): 17–32.

Bolancé, C., Guillen, M., and Nielsen, J. P. (2003). Kernel density estimation of actuarial loss functions. *Insurance: Mathematics and Economics*, 32 (1): 19–36.

Bolancé, C., Guillen, M., and Nielsen, J. P. (2008). Inverse beta transformation in kernel density estimation. *Statistics & Probability Letters*, 78 (13): 1757–1764.

Bolance, C., Guillen, M., Pelican, E., and Vernic, R. (2008). Skewed bivariate models and nonparametric estimation for the {CTE} risk measure. *Insurance: Mathematics and Economics*, 43 (3): 386–393.

Buch, A., Dorfleitner, G., and Wimmer, M. (2011). Risk capital allocation for RORAC optimization. *Journal of Banking and Finance*, 35 (11): 3001–3009.

Buch-Larsen, T., Nielsen, J. P., Guillen, M., and Bolancé, C. (2005). Kernel density estimation for heavy-tailed distributions using the champernowne transformation. *Statistics*, 39 (6): 503–516.

Cai, J. and Wei, W. (2014). Some new notions of dependence with applications in optimal allocations problems. *Insurance: Mathematics and Economics*, 55: 200–209.

Cerreia-Vioglio, S., Maccheroni, F., Marinacci, M., and Montrucchio, L. (2011). Risk measures: Rationality and diversification. *Mathematical Finance*, 21 (4): 743–774.

Chen, D., Mao, T., Pan, X., and Hu, T. (2012). Extreme value behavior of aggregate dependent risks. *Insurance: Mathematics and Economics*, 50 (1): 99–108.

Cheung, K. C. (2009). Upper comonotonicity. *Insurance: Mathematics and Economics*, 45 (1): 35–40.

Choquet, G. (1954). Theory of Capacities. *Annales de l'Institute Fourier*, 5: 131–295.

Cont, R., Deguest, R., and Scandolo, G. (2010). Robustness and sensitivity analysis of risk measurement procedures. *Quantitative Finance*, 10 (6): 593–606.

Cornish, E. A. and Fisher, R. A. (1937). Moments and cumulants in the specification of distributions. *Revue de l'Institut International de Statistique*, 4: 307–320.

Cossette, H., Côté, M., Marceau, E., and Moutanabbir, K. (2013). Multivariate distribution defined with Farlie-Gumbel-Morgenstern copula and mixed Erland marginals: Aggregation and capital allocation. *Insurance: Mathematics and Economics*, 52: 560–572.

Cossette, H., Mailhot, M., and Marceau, E. (2012). TVaR-based capital allocation for multivariate compound distributions with positive continuous claim amounts. *Insurance: Mathematics and Economics*, 50: 247–256.

Cox, L. A. T. (2012). Confronting deep uncertainties in risk analysis. *Risk Analysis*, 32 (10): 1607–1629.

Cox Jr., L.A. (2013). *Improving Risk Analysis*. Springer-Verlag New York.

Danielsson, J., Jorgensen, B. J., Sarma, M., and de Vries, C. G. (2005). Subadditivity re-examined: the case for Value-at-Risk. Technical report, CiteSeerx.

De Baets, B. (2013). Aggregation 2.0. Opening plenary session of the AGOP 2013 conference, Pamplona, Spain.

Degen, M., Lambrigger, D. D., and Segers, J. (2010). Risk concentration and diversification: Second-order properties. *Insurance: Mathematics and Economics*, 46 (3): 541–546.

Denault, M. (2001). Coherent allocation of risk capital. *Journal of Risk*, 4 (1): 1–34.

Denneberg, D. (1994). *Non-Additive Measure and Integral*. Kluwer Academic Publishers, Dordrecht.

Denuit, M., Dhaene, J., Goovaerts, M., and Kaas, R. (2005). *Actuarial Theory for Dependent Risks. Measures, Orders and Models*. John Wiley & Sons Ltd, Chichester.

Denuit, M., Dhaene, J., Goovaerts, M., Kaas, R., and Laeven, R. (2006). Risk measurement with equivalent utility principles. *Statistics & Decisions*, 24 (1): 1–25.

Dhaene, J., Kukush, A., Linders, D., and Tang, Q. (2012a). Remarks on quantiles and distortion risk measures. *European Actuarial Journal*, 2 (2): 319–328.

Dhaene, J., Laeven, R. J. A., Vanduffel, S., Darkiewicz, G., and Goovaerts, M. J. (2008). Can a coherent risk measure be too subadditive? *Journal of Risk and Insurance*, 75 (2): 365–386.

Dhaene, J., Tsanakas, A., Valdez, E. A., and Vanduffel, S. (2012b). Optimal capital allocation principles. *Journal of Risk and Insurance*, 79 (1): 1–28.

Dujmović, J. J. (2006). A comparison of andness/orness indicators. *In: Proceedings of the 11th Information Processing and Management of Uncertainty international (IPMU 2006)*, pages 691–698.

Ekeland, I., Galichon, A., and Henry, M. (2012). Comonotonic measures of multivariate risks. *Mathematical Finance*, 22 (1): 109–132.

Embrechts, P., Lambrigger, D. D., and Wuethrich, M. V. (2009a). Multivariate extremes and the aggregation of dependent risks: examples and counterexamples. *Extremes*, 12 (2): 107–127.

Embrechts, P., Liu, H., and Wang, R. (2016). Quantile-based Risk Sharing. Technical report, RiskLab - ETH and Department of Statistics and Actuarial Science, University of Waterloo.

Embrechts, P., Neslehova, J., and Wuethrich, M. V. (2009b). Additivity properties for Value-at-Risk under Archimedean dependence and heavy-tailedness. *Insurance: Mathematics and Economics*, 44 (2, SI): 164–169.

Fernández Salido, J. and Murakami, S. (2003). Extending Yager's orness concept for the OWA aggregators to other mean operators. *Fuzzy Sets and Systems*, 139 (3): 515–542.

Fisher, R. A. and Cornish, E. A. (1960). The percentile points of distributions having known cumulants. *Technometrics*, 2 (2): 209–225.

Föllmer, H. and Schied, A. (2002). Convex measures of risk and trading constraints. *Finance and Stochastics*, 6 (4): 429–447.

Frittelli, M. and Rosazza Gianin, E. (2002). Putting order in risk measures. *Journal of Banking & Finance*, 26 (7): 1473–1486.

Furman, E. and Landsman, Z. (2006). Tail variance premium with applications for elliptical portfolio of risks. *ASTIN Bulletin*, 36 (2): 433–462.

Giamouridis, D. (2006). Estimation risk in financial risk management: A correction. *Journal of Risk*, 8 (4): 121–125.

Goovaerts, M., Linders, D., Van Weert, K., and Tank, F. (2012). On the interplay between distortion, mean value and Haezendonck-Goovaerts risk measures. *Insurance: Mathematics and Economics*, 51 (1): 10–18.

Goovaerts, M. J., Kaas, R., and Laeven, R. J. (2010). A note on additive risk measures in rank-dependent utility. *Insurance: Mathematics and Economics*, 47 (2): 187–189.

Grechuk, B., Molyboha, A., and Zabarankin, M. (2012). Mean-deviation analysis in the theory of choice. *Risk Analysis*, 32 (8): 1277–1292.

Grégoire, P. (2007). *Advanced Portfolio Attribution Analysis: New Approaches to Return and Risk*. Riskbooks, Incisive Media.

Guillen, M., Bolancé, C., and Santolino, M. (2016). Fundamentals of Risk Measurement and Aggregation for Insurance Applications. *In:* Torra, V., Narukawa, Y., Navarro-Arribas, G., and Yañez, C., editors, *Modeling Decisions for Artificial Intelligence MDAI 2016*, pages 15–25. Springer, Hidelberg.

Guillen, M., Prieto, F., and Sarabia, J. M. (2011). Modelling losses and locating the tail with the pareto positive stable distribution. *Insurance: Mathematics and Economics*, 49 (3): 454–461.

Guillen, M., Sarabia, J. M., and Prieto, F. (2013). Simple risk measure calculations for sums of positive random variables. *Insurance: Mathematics and Economics*, 53 (1): 273–280.

Hosking, J. and Wallis, J. (1987). Parameter and quantile estimation for the generalized Pareto distribution. *Technometrics*, 29 (3): 339–349.

Hua, L. and Joe, H. (2012). Tail comonotonicity: Properties, constructions, and asymptotic additivity of risk measures. *Insurance: Mathematics and Economics*, 51 (2): 492–503.

Hürlimann, W. (2006). A note on generalized distortion risk measures. *Finance Reseach Letters*, 3 (4): 267–272.

Jiang, L. (2008). Convexity, translation invariance and subadditivity for g-expectations and related risk measures. *Annals of Applied Probability*, 18 (1): 245–258.

Johnson, N. L. and Kotz, S. (1970). *Distributions in Statistics: Continuous Univariate Distributions - 1*. John Wiley & Sons, New York.

Kalkbrener, M. (2005). An axiomatic approach to capital allocation. *Mathematical Finance*, 15 (3): 425–437.

Kaluszka, M. and Krzeszowiec, M. (2012). Pricing insurance contracts under cumulative prospect theory. *Insurance: Mathematics and Economics*, 50 (1): 159–166.

Li, X. and You, Y. (2015). Permutation monotone functions of random vectors with applications in financial and actuarial risk management. *Advances in Applied Probability*, 47 (1): 270–291.

Lv, W., Pan, X., and Hu, T. (2013). Asymptotics of the risk concentration based on the tail distortion risk measure. *Statistics and Probability Letters*, 83 (12): 2703–2710.

MacKenzie, C. A. (2014). Summarizing risk using risk measures and risk indices. *Risk analysis*, 34 (12): 2143–2162.

McCune, E. and Gray, H. (1982). Cornish-Fisher and Edgeworth expansions. *In:* Samuel Kotz and Norman L. Johnson, editor, *Encyclopedia of Statistical Sciences*, volume 2. John Wiley & Sons, New York.

McNeil, A. J., Frey, R., and Embrechts, P. (2005). *Quantitative Risk Management*. Princeton Series in Finance. Princeton University Press, New York.

Nam, H. S., Tang, Q., and Yang, F. (2011). Characterization of upper comonotonicity via tail convex order. *Insurance: Mathematics and Economics*, 48 (3): 368–373.

Overbeck, L. (2000). *Measuring Risk in Complex Systems*. Springer.

Rahl, L., editor (2012). *Risk Budgeting: Risk Appetite and Governance in the Wake of the Financial Crisis*. Riskbooks, Incisive Media, 2nd edition.

Rüschendorf, L. (2013). *Mathematical Risk Analysis. Dependence, Risk Bounds, Optimal Allocation and Portfolios*. Springer Series in Operations Research and Financial Engineering. Springer-Verlag, Berlin Heidelberg.

Sandström, A. (2007). Solvency II: Calibration for skewness. *Scandinavian Actuarial Journal*, 2: 126–134.

Sandström, A. (2011). *Handbook of Solvency for Actuaries and Risk Managers. Theory and Practice*. CRC Finance Series. Chapman & Hall / CRC, Boca Raton.

Song, Y. and Yan, J.-A. (2009). Risk measures with comonotonic subadditivity or convexity and respecting stochastic orders. *Insurance: Mathematics and Economics*, 45 (3): 459–465.

Tasche, D. (1999). Risk contributions and performance measurement. Working paper, Lehrstuhl für Mathematische Statistik, TU München.

Tasche, D. (2004). *Economic Capital: A Practitioner's Guide*. Risk Books, IncisiveMedia.

Tasche, D. (2007). Euler allocation: Theory and practice. Working paper.

Torra, V. and Narukawa, Y. (2007). *Modeling Decisions: Information Fusion and Aggregation Operators*. Springer, Berlin.

Tsanakas, A. (2009). To split or not to split: Capital allocation with convex risk measures. *Insurance: Mathematics and Economics*, 44 (2): 268–277.

Tsanakas, A. and Desli, E. (2005). Measurement and pricing of risk in insurance markets. *Risk Analysis*, 25 (6): 1653–1668.

Tsanakas, A. and Millossovich, P. (2016). Sensitivity analysis using risk measures. *Risk Analysis*, 36 (1): 30–48.

Urbina, J. and Guillen, M. (2014). An application of capital allocation principles to operational risk and the cost of fraud. *Expert Systems with Applications*, 41 (16): 7023–7031.

van Gulick, G., De Waegenaere, A., and Norde, H. (2012). Excess based allocation of risk capital. *Insurance: Mathematics and Economics*, 50 (1): 26–42.

Wang, M. (2014). Capital allocation based on the tail covariance premium adjusted. *Insurance: Mathematics and Economics*, 57: 125–131.

Wang, S. S. (1995). Insurance pricing and increased limits ratemaking by proportional hazard transforms. *Insurance: Mathematics and Economics*, 17 (1): 43–54.

Wang, S. S. (1996). Premium calculation by transforming the layer premium density. *ASTIN Bullletin*, 26 (1): 71–92.

Wang, S. S. (1998). An actuarial index of the right-tail risk. *North American Actuarial Journal*, 2 (2): 88–101.

Wang, S. S. (2002). A risk measure that goes beyond coherence. *In: Proceedings of the 2002 AFIR (Actuarial approach to financial risks)*.

Wang, S. S. and Dhaene, J. (1998). Comonotonicity, correlation order and premium principles. *Insurance: Mathematics and Economics*, 22 (3): 235–242.

Wirch, J. L. and Hardy, M. R. (2002). Distortion risk measures: Coherence and stochastic dominance. IME Conference, Lisbon.

Wu, X. Y. and Zhou, X. (2006). A new characterization of distortion premiums via countable additivity for comonotonic risks. *Insurance: Mathematics and Economics*, 38 (2): 324–334.

Xu, M. and Hu, T. (2012). Stochastic comparisons of capital allocations with applications. *Insurance: Mathematics and Economics*, 50 (3): 293–298.

Xu, M. and Mao, T. (2013). Optimal capital allocation based on the Tail Mean-Variance model. *Insurance: Mathematics and Economics*, 53: 533–543.

Yaari, M. E. (1987). The dual theory of choice under risk. *Econometrica*, 55 (1): 95–115.

You, Y. and Li, X. (2014). Optimal capital allocations to interdependent actuarial risks. *Insurance: Mathematics and Economics*, 57: 104–113.

Zaks, Y. and Tsanakas, A. (2014). Optimal capital allocation in a hierarchical corporate structure. *Insurance: Mathematics and Economics*, 56: 48–55.

Zhu, L. and Li, H. (2012). Tail distortion risk and its asymptotic analysis. *Insurance: Mathematics and Economics*, 51 (1): 115–121.

Biographies of the authors

Jaume Belles-Sampera holds a PhD in Business and a Master in Mathematics from the University of Barcelona (UB). Since 2015 he works at Grupo Catalana Occidente (GCO) as member of the department in charge of the actuarial function of this international insurance group. His main research interests are capital allocation, risk measures and aggregation functions. He is member of the UB Riskcenter. He was awarded with the 'Ferran Armengol i Tubau' prize from the Catalan Society of Economy in its 2014 edition, for his contributions on the analysis of risk measures in insurance and financial applications. He is a certified Financial Risk Manager (FRM) from the Global Association of Risk Professionals (GARP).

Montserrat Guillen received a Master of Science in Mathematics and Mathematical Statistics and a PhD in Economics from the University of Barcelona in 1992. She received a MSc in Data Analysis from the University of Essex (United Kingdom). Since 2001 she is Chair Professor of the Department of Econometrics at the University of Barcelona. She is currently Honorary Visiting Professor in the Faculty of Actuarial Science and Insurance at City University London. She was Visiting Research faculty at the University of Texas at Austin (USA) and Visiting Professor of Insurance Econometrics at the University of Paris II. She was awarded the ICREA Academia distinction. She is an associate editor for the Journal of Risk and Insurance, a senior editor of Astin Bulletin, co-editor for the North American Actuarial Journal and was chief editor until 2014 (now associate editor) of SORT-Statistics and Operations Research Transactions.

Miguel Santolino is associate professor, and director of the Master program in Actuarial and Financial Sciences at the University of Barcelona (UB). He holds a PhD in Business Studies, MA Actuarial Science and MA Economics from the UB and MSc in Financial and Actuarial Engineering from the Katholieke Universiteit Leuven (Belgium). His research focuses on the analysis and evaluation of risk, including the design of new risk measures, the mechanisms for the resolution of disputes, including Alternative Dispute Resolution (ADR) methods, and the investigation of motor accidents to design adequate road safety policies.

Index